# Military Airfields of Cambridgeshire

From Alconbury to Wyton, an illustrated guide
to the histories of all thirty military
airfields in Cambridgeshire.

# ACTION STATIONS
## Military Airfields of
# Cambridgeshire

### Michael J.F. Bowyer

**Patrick Stephens**
**Wellingborough, Northamptonshire**

© Michael J. F. Bowyer 1987
All rights reserved. No part of this publication may
be reproduced or utilized in any form or by any means,
electronic or mechanical, including photocopying,
recording or by any information storage and retrieval
system, without permission in writing from the Publisher.

First published 1987

*British Library Cataloguing in Publication Data*

Action stations.
Military airfields of Cambridgeshire
1. Great Britain. *Royal Air Force* —
History    2. Air bases — Great Britain
— History
1. Bowyer, Michael J.F.
358.4'17'0941        UG635.G72

ISBN 0-85059-823-0

**Cover illustrations:**
**Front:** *Stirling Mk 1 of No 1651 Conversion Unit, Waterbeach.* **Back:** *Mosquito XVI of 571 Squadron, Oakington.*

*Patrick Stephens is part of the
Thorsons Publishing Group*

Printed and bound in Great Britain

# CONTENTS

# INTRODUCTION

*Action Stations 1* appeared in 1979 and soon one major problem became apparent, the future need to update the contents. Even a small insertion would demand an entirely new layout of the contents. Eventually it was decided that the easiest solution would be to update and perhaps expand sections of the series on a county basis where warranted. This volume is the first in a new range, and presents much that is fresh concerning the airfields of Cambridgeshire.

It highlights the utter stupidity of combining areas with total economic and agricultural differences whilst failing to tackle intelligently the administrative problem of small market towns, originally sited to be within a day's walking distance apart. Newmarket Heath airfield straddled the county boundary, but since Newmarket itself is of Suffolk its airfield has not been included. Molesworth, Alconbury and Upwood so clearly belong to a region beyond Cambridgeshire and by the time a Cambridge traveller reaches Wittering the landscape is obviously part of the East Midlands. Re-alignment of boundaries during the rule of Edward Heath extended the real Cambridgeshire and produced a most unattractive, illogical, political concoction whose area forms the basis for the contents of this volume.

To many a stranger Cambridgeshire is regarded as a flat, featureless expanse with little to commend a visit. Nothing could be further from the truth for the higher chalk ground, forming the southern third and which sweeps across the county from Royston to Newmarket, is highly attractive at all seasons. The Cam Valley is nothing like its name implies and its river rises in undulating ground which forms much of the west of the county whose north-west region — once Huntingdonshire — is quite hilly. Only to the north of Cambridge is the ground flat, with magnificent cloudscapes as compensation and a giant openess reminiscent of parts of Africa.

During the war, few, if any counties, could have witnessed more varied, intense air activity than 'Cambridgeshire'. Bombers in profusion, fighters, trainers, transports — British and later American — flew from and over the area. Autogiros milled their ways out of Duxford and even flying boats were not an infrequent sight. Indeed, one landed close to Cambridge! The latest types were there to be seen, glider trains chugged over in swarms. A fine morning would bring hundreds of vapour trails as the 8th Air Force set forth for the fight. Soon clear, the skies would then be packed with our own bombers being air tested or training their crews.

So intensive was the amount of flying that in 1942 Fighter

Command ordered the Observer Corps to gather — only over Cambridgeshire — detailed census figures for an assessment of the effectiveness of flying control over such a busy area.

So many airfields in a small space made the region very attractive to the enemy and from mid-1940 to mid-1944 the Luftwaffe waged an intruder campaign. That its scope was reduced from 1941 was an act of enormous folly, for even a handful of intruders could have brought vast disruption at dawn, dusk and during darkness. Some measure of the extent of these operations can be judged from the recently published volume *Air Raid!* (Patrick Stephens).

Many readers of *Action Stations 1* have contacted us since its publication. Nevertheless there remain squadrons and units based in the county for which few if any photographs seem to have survived, squadrons like 35, 168, 142, 156, 157 and units such as 22 EFTS and the Pathfinder NTU among them. May I ask if you do have any such photographs, to please contact us for the sight of a rare picture gives so much pleasure to so many. Who knows, we may one day be able to include them in an update of this volume!

## Acknowledgements

*Action Stations: Cambridgeshire* has benefitted much from the help of two increasingly better known Cambridgeshire institutions. One is the Cambridgeshire Collection held in Cambridge Central Library. Master-minded by Michael Petty, it has an increasing aviation content from which I have gratefully been able to draw. The other is the County Record Office in Shire Hall, Castle Hill. There, Michael Farrar and his staff maintain in particular 'official' records. Included is microfilm of local RAF wartime squadron histories, some of which would otherwise need to be consulted in Kew's Public Record Office. They are a facility that should be more widely used. To the staff of both collections I extend my thanks for always being extremely helpful.

Books such as this invariably are the result of decades of harvesting. The origins of many items would be difficult to place. Easily identifiable is the assistance of Reginald Mack and the RAF Museum, Marshall Engineering of Cambridge and the Imperial War Museum who have supplied photographs. The US Air Force, Peter Green and Andrew Thomas also made generous contributions.

In particular, my thanks, very long overdue, may here be most conveniently expressed to a local team who in their youth may well have formed the nation's most ardent 'total aviation persons' set. Of them, Donald Mee quite clearly heading for the aviation heights had just joined the technical sales team of Britain's most glittering aircraft when he was so tragically taken from us. His close companion, Malcolm Hayward, has spent his working life at Hatfield from where all post-Comet creations carry part of his academic expertise. No Tornado passes without the aid of Mick Jeffries who from the 1940s was 'engine crazy'! From our little group and via Turbo Union and the RB 199 he joined the mighty, travelling via the RB 211 to become Rolls-Royce leader on TriStar at Lockheed before becoming part of the team devising the new, mighty Pratt & Whitney 'civil' engine.

Nothing settled on Mr Marshall's giant lawn in the 1940s and early '50s without Gerald Lawrance and John Stacey rushing the news to me. Gerald it was who rattled the door knocker calling 'the civil Spitfire is flying', or 'a Bristol Freighter has landed, Mike', and he was always getting us all excited. Gerald's love of all flying things remains as strong as ever and in more recent years it has been encouraged, like mine, by John Strangward ever the fount of 'the latest' news.

To my friend of most long-standing, Alan Wright, whose *Civil Aircraft Markings* is flashed upon airport roofs and where ever the civilised enthusiasts gather, my gratitude is massive. The magic aviation moments and comradeship that we have shared are beyond number.

All have contributed massively to all that I have ever written, for my role from very early childhood has been that of the chronicler privileged to suggest and record, greatly encouraged by grand friends close at hand.


Michael J.F. Bowyer                                    November 1986
Cambridge

# MAPS

Airfields in the following four maps are numbered in accordance with the sequence given in the list below:

| | | | |
|---|---|---|---|
| 1 | Alconbury | 16 | Mepal |
| 2 | Bassingbourn | 17 | Molesworth |
| 3 | Bottisham | 18 | Oakington |
| 4 | Bourn | 19 | Peterborough (Westwood) |
| 5 | Cambridge | 20 | Sibson |
| 6 | Castle Camps | 21 | Snailwell |
| 7 | Caxton Gibbet | 22 | Somersham |
| 8 | Duxford | 23 | Steeple Morden |
| 9 | Fowlmere | 24 | Upwood |
| 10 | Glatton | 25 | Warboys |
| 11 | Gransden Lodge | 26 | Waterbeach |
| 12 | Graveley | 27 | Witchford |
| 13 | Kimbolton | 28 | Wittering |
| 14 | Little Staughton | 29 | Wratting Common |
| 15 | Lord's Bridge | 30 | Wyton |

## Key

- Self-accounting / parent / main airfield.
- Satellite airfield.
- Relief Landing Ground (RLG).

The letters following airfield numbers indicate: AC — Army Co-operation Command station; B — bomber station; F — fighter station; T — training station; US — United States Army Air Force base.

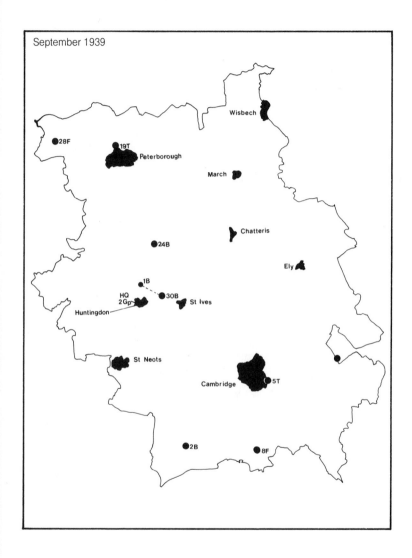

September 1939

Wisbech

●28F

19T
Peterborough

March

Chatteris

●24B

Ely

1B
HQ
2Gp
●30B St Ives
Huntingdon

St Neots

Cambridge
5T

●2B

●8F

*Eight airfields in use on 3 September 1939. Main towns are shown, and Newmarket Heath airfield on the county border.*

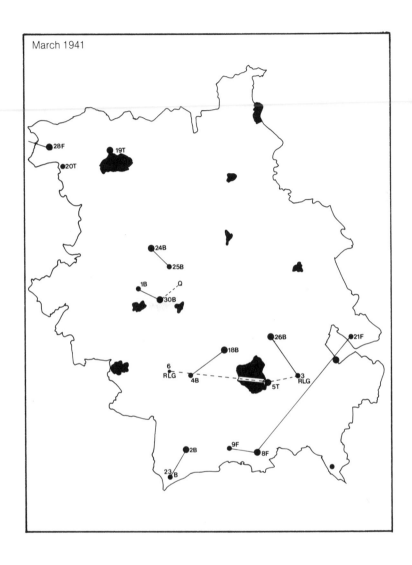

March 1941

March 1941 and eighteen airfields are in use. Satellites are linked to parents, Cambridge to RLGs. Somersham remains a Q-Site.

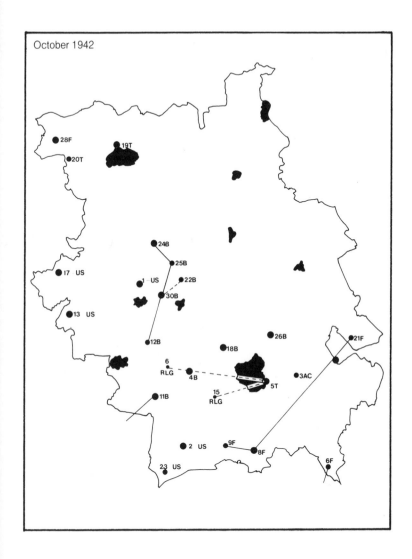

October 1942

October 1942 and 25 airfields are in use. Bomber stations are mainly for Pathfinders, and the USAF uses five bases.

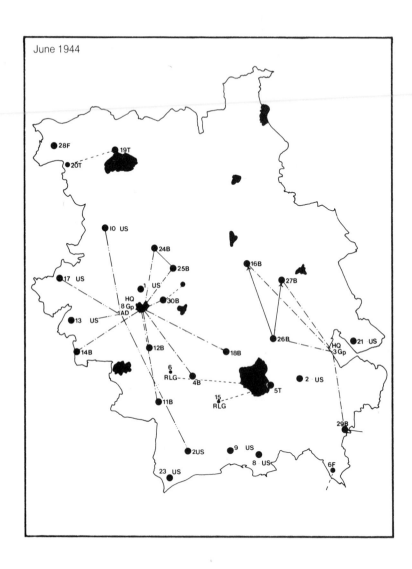

June 1944

*6 June and thirty airfields are available. RAF bomber stations are controlled by 3 Group HQ, Exning or 8 Group HQ, Huntingdon. 1st Air Division, USAAF, Brampton, controls four Bombardment Groups and the USAAF uses six more airfields.*

14

# THE AIRFIELDS

## Alconbury

*TL213768. By the A14 5 miles NW Huntingdon*

Oakington was a quagmire, its photo-reconnaissance Spitfires of 3 PRU needing a firmer surface from which to operate. Alconbury became the chosen alternative from where, on 30 January 1941, a new phase in the airfield's history commenced when Flying Officer J. H. R. Blount set off to photograph Hamburg and Flying Officer Hood headed for Gelsenkirchen, each courageously alone in a PR Spitfire Type C. Similar operations followed, when the weather allowed, and on 14 March came the highlight. Squadron Leader P. B. B. Ogilvie in Spitfire *X4712* left Alconbury at 09:45, took on twenty gallons of fuel at Horsham St Faith and at 12:25 arrived over Berlin, thereby being the first Allied airman to reach 'the Big City' in daylight. It was a stupendous effort, for, when he landed back at Alconbury at 14:40 with 25 superb photographs, only twenty gallons of fuel remained in the Spitfire's tanks.

Alconbury is reckoned to have been the first used satellite landing ground for a main RAF station. Prior to hostilities it was usual to place aircraft in hangars at the end of the working day. Fear of air attack in wartime led to their being dispersed around airfield perimeters, camouflaging taking place when possible although netting aircraft was difficult. With perhaps forty aircraft on one aerodrome, grass dispersal zones became crowded, for 1939 airfields were usually quite small. Dispersing them to a suitable field site nearby was a 1938 idea. Whilst re-arming there was feasible, also crew briefing, main overhauls and battle repair would have to be undertaken at the parent station. By summer 1940 some squadrons were entirely based at satellites, and a new use had been devised. By concentrating night flying at the lit primitive satellite, the main station would receive less enemy attention. Gradually, many satellites developed into self-accounting RAF stations — as was the case with Alconbury.

Land for this satellite was acquired in 1938 just north of Alconbury village on the hill top, a large grass field to which, on 17–18 May 1938, Battles of 63 Squadron, Upwood, were dispersed, crews being accommodated under canvas in operational conditions whilst the first trials of the satellite system were undertaken.

When war came Alconbury at once was used, but not for Upwood's squadrons since they were now non-operational. Instead, it became Wyton's satellite and Blenheims were dispersed there. As soon as Norway was invaded Wyton's Blenheim squadrons were placed on high alert, and late afternoon on 14 April 1940 XV Squadron moved completely to Alconbury. There it awaited orders, personnel returning to Wyton each night. No call came — until the Germans invaded the Low Countries on 10 May. Mid-morning that day two Blenheims left Alconbury to reconnoitre the state of river bridges in the Low Countries. At 14:15 nine more took off, to attack Waalhaven airfield south of Rotterdam. Once home their serious battle damage needed repair, then XV Squadron stood by to operate on 12 May. The result was disastrous.

Vital to the halting of the German advance was the destruction of a bridge at Maastricht in Holland. Twelve Blenheims, 36 men of XV Squadron, set off. Only half returned, and one of those crash landed. The squadron had only two serviceable Blenheims left — and eighteen empty places in the Messes. A massacre had occurred and the remnants of the proud squadron were absorbed by 40 Squadron at Wyton for resumption of operations. Losses throughout 2 Group were to become horrific over the next few weeks, and not until June 1940 was XV Squadron fully

*40 Squadron Wellington 1cs at Alconbury in 1941.*

established again at Alconbury to fight with enormous courage throughout the summer. Something of what this and other squadrons endured can be read in *2 Group RAF* (Faber & Faber).

On 1 November 1940, XV and 40 Squadrons and their stations were switched to No 3 (Bomber) Group. Rapidly re-armed with Wellington Ics, they trained for Main Force night raids. Alconbury's Blenheim crews had some experience of those, having participated in ferocious attacks on barges massing in the Channel ports for the invasion of Britain. No XV Squadron's Wellingtons first went into action, from Alconbury, on 22 December. In February 1941 after mounting eleven raids, XV Squadron was replaced by 40 Squadron, XV having moved to Wyton to re-arm with Stirlings.

Between arrival at Alconbury and late November 1941, when much of 40 Squadron went overseas, its Wellingtons flew 713 operational sorties from which 23 aircraft did not return. Another five crashed in the course of operations. There were many moments of drama in those months during which the squadron attacked Germany many times. On 2/3 September, for instance, with Frankfurt the target, *R1030* 'R-Robert' had an engine failure when over the sea. To the moment of ditching Sergeant Robertson, the wireless operator, stayed at his post sending messages requesting help until the moment of impact. A trawler man-

aged to rescue four of the crew, but Pilot Officer Fitch, the pilot who had skilfully ditched the 'Wimpey', and his wireless operator, were both drowned.

On dark nights homing was never easy, radio aids being quite primitive. Sergeant Jenner and crew reached and bombed Berlin, but as if that task was not bad enough they became lost over England during their nine-hour flight. Eventually *R1331* — also an 'R-Robert' — crashed into a hill near Combe Martin, Devon. Sergeant Griffin, the rear gunner, baled out too low and was killed, but the others miraculously survived. A remaining echelon of 40 Squadron continued to operate from Alconbury between 27 November and 14 February 1942 when it was re-numbered 156 Squadron after it had flown 69 sorties in the course of nineteen operations. Five days later the new squadron received its first Hercules-powered Wellington III, first operating with that version on 25 March although Mk Ics were retained throughout its Alconbury stay.

The squadron operated from Alconbury for the three '1,000 bomber' raids, carried out mining and gradually slipped into a marker role dropping flares and incendiaries during rudimentary target marking. There were many instances when extreme courage was called for. On 23 July Flight Sergeant T. E. Case had to take sudden evasive action when another Wellington closed upon him.

Some of his incendiaries caught fire and Warrant Officer McLennan saved the aircraft by picking up burning bombs and pushing these and magazines through the aircraft's fabric even though he had no gloves on his hands. During a Bremen raid of 27 July a Wellington was coned by searchlights, anti-aircraft fire shooting away the port elevator and injuring some of the crew. The second pilot took over at the Dutch coast and the remainder of the crew decided to bale out, leaving the second pilot to land successfully at Colti-shall, a very fine effort.

Between formation and 6/7 August 1942 No 156 Squadron mounted 62 operations, flew 386 sorties and lost fourteen aircraft. It first engaged in mine-laying on 16 April and in July flew two daylight 'Moling' raids against north-west Germany. In August 1942 the Pathfinder Force formed and 156 Squadron moved on 5-7 August to nearby Warboys and into the marker force. The reason for the move? The Americans were coming.

Come they did in August 1942 and early in September the first B-24 Libera-tors to be based in Britain arrived, forming the 93rd Bomb Group. With high aspect ratio wings the B-24s were immediately recognisable. The Americans were rar-ing to go into action, and when one talked with them one sensed that they did not understand that it could be a dangerous activity, and knew nothing of the torture endured by Alconbury's Blenheim crews.

The 93rd entered combat on 9 October. Five formations were laid on against Target Z183, the Fives-Lille steel works, including B-17s of the 301st Bomb Group leading followed by twelve of the 11th CCRG with 24 B-17s of the 306th. Then came 24 B-24s of the 93rd and bringing up the rear 24 B-17s of the 97th Bomb Group, so that the Liberators had rear cover in the largest American raid so far.

Take-off from Alconbury was around 08:30 hours, on a fine, sunny autumn morning. It was exciting to see the B-24s taking up battle stations over Cambridge against a sky crossed by countless vapour trails. Then they headed for Felix-stowe where the entire force made ren-dezvous. They flew south, meeting two squadrons of RAF Spitfire IXs, then three squadrons of USAAF P-38 Lightnings five miles east of Dunkirk. Further east was a formation of 'Moonshine' Defiants of 515 Squadron attempting to jam enemy radar and screen the bombers.

The bombers flew directly to Fives-Lille meeting three more squadrons of RAF Spitfire IXs giving target support to ward off attacks on the 93rd and 306th Bomb Groups, both inexperienced. Ger-man reaction was fierce. A B-24 was shot down, ten were damaged and bombing was poor. Only nine bombs fell within a quarter of a mile of the target, many homes being destroyed. When the evening news bulletin revealed the oper-ation, American claims of 48 enemy fighters shot down and 38 probables were unbelievable. Post-war research suggests that only one fighter was des-troyed. One thing was certain, the B-24 crews discovered that combat was no joyride.

B-24 spares at Alconbury were in short supply, the aircraft needing many modifi-cations, but operations continued with the bombing of La Pallice, Brest, St Nazaire and Lorient. A new task was soon set the 93rd. With convoys sailing for North-West Africa it was essential air cover be provided over Biscay. The 93rd left Alconbury to provide this, the Libera-tor being ideal for a maritime role.

Although the 93rd moved to the Middle East in December 1942, many Ameri-cans remained at Alconbury where, in January 1943, B-17s of the 92nd Bomb Group arrived. Mostly early B-17Es, they retained their striking mid-1942 style unusual camouflage. The 95th Bomb Group passed through in summer and on 19 June Alconbury became Station 102, US 8th Air Force. The 92nd left for Podington mid-September 1943 leaving behind an Alconbury which had three runways — 24/06 of 1,925 yd and two of

*Alconbury RF-4C AR/64-081, summer 1975.*

1,400 yd, two 'T2' hangars and fifty loop hardstandings. Accommodation for over 400 officers and nearly 2,500 other ranks was available.

August 1943 saw the arrival of the 482nd Bomb Group on the 23rd, its task to provide pathfinding leadships for the offensive. Three squadrons flew B-17Fs, the fourth B-24s, all of which were fitted with blind bombing devices. These aircraft preceded bomber formations to mark targets when cloud covered, flying their first missions on 27 September 1943 and leading the 1st and 3rd Air Divisions to Emden. Later, their aircraft were detached to other bases, to attack, for instance, factories at Gotha, Schweinfurt and Brunswick.

In March 1944 the 482nd came off operations to organize a pathfinder school at Alconbury. They made radar photographs of enemy territory, tested radar and guided H2S into service. For this purpose they flew a few Mosquito PR XVIs which used to disperse in the southwest corner of the field with the Dominie, Norseman and Cessna Bobcat used for communications.

Sometimes the Group operated as on D-Day when it led attacks on enemy traffic. The mixture of trials and training with some operations continued to the end of the war, the 482nd leaving for America in May–June 1945. Alconbury quietened and returned to the RAF on 26 November 1945.

It remained inactive until 1 June 1953 when the Americans returned. US Congress had agreed to fund a 9,000-ft runway and modernization of the airfield over a two-year period. Republic F-84s from Manston would move here in the event of war, otherwise Alconbury would be a USAF Air Depot. The 7523rd Squadron set to and in March 1955 the 7560th Air Base Group, 3rd AF, was activated. On 15 September 1955 the 85th Bomb Squadron, 47th Bomb Wing, arrived from Sculthorpe with North American B-45A jet bombers. During its stay the 85th converted to Douglas B-66Bs and between May and August 1959 was accompanied by the 53rd Weather Squadron's WB-50Ds.

The departure of the 85th was a result of the French being unwilling to accommodate US forces. A general rearrangement followed, the 10th Tactical Reconnaissance Wing arriving on 25 August 1959 from Spangdahlem, Germany. They brought RB-66s, the 1st and 30th Squadrons taking up residence at Alconbury. In May 1965 the Wing began

*A sinister and sophisticated TR-1 at Alconbury in the 1980s.*

to equip with RF-4C Phantom IIs which until 1987 the 1st TRS flew from Alconbury. On 1 April 1976 the 30th Squadron was deactivated, as the 527th Tactical Fighter Training Aggressor Squadron formed to act as targets for many NATO organizations. They received their first Northrop F-5E Tiger IIs in May 1976 and became fully operational on 1 January 1977.

Tiger IIs remain active at Alconbury, but their presence has been overshadowed by the arrival of jet black spooky-looking Lockheed TR-1 tactical surveillance aircraft. Successor to the famed U-2, this sailplane-like machine, almost inaudible, carries super-sophisticated radar and sensors allowing very high altitude surveillance well away from any ground fighting zone. The first of the TR-1s, which equip the 95th Reconnaissance Squadron of the 17th Reconnaissance Wing, arrived on 12 February 1983.

# Bassingbourn

*TL330460. On A14 4 miles N of Royston, Herts*

In the moonlight Wellingtons were flying the usual round of circuits and bumps, or setting off on cross-country journeys. Bassingbourn was the home of the most easterly bomber Operational Training Unit, No 11, the easiest within strike of the enemy who rightly assessed that crews in training were easy game.

In from the Wash crept Lietnant Heinz Völker, flying Ju 88C2 *842:R4+BL* of NJG 2 from Gilze Rijen in Holland. Wellington *R1334* had just taken off when the '88 closed, and to the west of the airfield its pilot opened fire. The Wellington swerved as the German aircraft turned and they collided. There was a tremendous explosion and a brilliant flash. For the eleven men the end was all but instantaneous as the mangled wreckage fell at Ashwell, making 22 July 1941 a night to remember.

Bassingbourn attracted several intruder attacks. On 10 April 1941 a Wellington I, *L4253*, was shot down near Ashwell and a fortnight later a further Wellington was brought down on a dispersal. On 7 May one was shot down during landing approach and in August yet another was destroyed north-east of Barrington - not far from Lord's Bridge bomb dump.

Bassingbourn opened in March 1938

*Bassingbourn Blenheim* L1203 *of 108 Squadron.*

and Hinds of 104 and 108 Squadrons moved in as part of 2 Group even before building of the four 'C' Type hangars was complete, let alone the mock Georgian buildings. The hangars, in the early days, were left as bare concrete, disguised only by saplings alongside. Early in 1939 large brown nets were slung across the hangars, and camouflage painting followed when war came.

During May–June 1938 the two squadrons were equipped with Blenheim Is, and in May 1939 23 Avro Ansons supplemented them assisting in the training of Volunteer Reserve aircrew. In September 1939 both became training units for 2 Group, and moved out to Bicester. They were replaced on 24 September 1939 by Wellingtons of 215 Squadron, a training unit for 3 Group. Severe drainage problems made a quagmire of parts of the airfield.

Early in December 1939 three Flights of Battle bombers of 35 Squadron arrived from Cranfield. Their role was the training of aircrew for the Advanced Air Striking

*Wellington N2912 arrived in April 1940 after operating with 99 Squadron. A Ju 88C intruder destroyed it over Bassingbourn on 24 April 1941 (IWM).*

Force in France. Brief was their stay for at the start of February 1940 they moved to Upwood.

Dispersals were built between the aged elms of Wimpole Park. As the Ansons went into hiding, traffic on the Old North Road halted to let them cross. No 215 Squadron dissolved, to become 11 OTU in April 1940.

Leaflet dropping by Wellingtons commenced on 21/22 July. On 5 November 1940 Whitleys of 10 and 78 Squadrons set off from Bassingbourn for Italy. The first bombs fell on the station on 28 November. The most memorable bombing came on 16 January 1941 when a huge bomb fell close to the main road not far from the water tower, leaving a giant crater twenty feet deep and fifty feet across.

Wellington Ics progressively replaced earlier variants. In December 1941 runway building commenced causing 11 OTU to move temporarily into Steeple Morden satellite and to Tempsford. At this time 54 Wellingtons, eleven Ansons and two Lysanders were at 11 OTU. On 24 April 1942 the first runway at Bassingbourn opened and 11 OTU filtered back, in time for the '1,000 bomber' raids. Twelve Wellingtons set off from Bassing-

bourn for the 1942 '1,000 bomber' raid on Cologne from which *R1065* never returned. Against Essen on 1/2 June eleven operated and twelve set out for Bremen on 25/26 June when two were missing. The Wellingtons participated in other Main Force operations, attacking Düsseldorf during the *Grand National* of 31 July and Bremen on 13/14 September. Between 28 September and 2 October 1942 11 OTU moved to Westcott.

In September news spread fast; the Americans were coming. It could be that the rumour was founded by chance for the first American aircraft was C-47 *7820*, ex-Chelveston, which set down in a hurry on 3 August. Flying over the Grantchester heavy gun battery it was not recognised, failed to fire the colour of the day and was fired upon, the crew hastening to safety at Bassingbourn. It was, however, 14 October 1942 when the Americans arrived in B-17Fs of the 91st Bomb Group, some of the first '17Fs to arrive in Britain.

In November they commenced bombing missions. Submarine pens, shipyards, docks, airfields, factories and communications targets, all were attacked. The 91st Bomb Group took part

*'Watch what you say, Mr Hope, the locals ...!' Bob Hpe and Colonel Hare in Bassingbourn's Officers' Club, 7 July 1943* (US Air Force).

**Above** *B-17Fs ('Rebel's Revenge' nearest) of the 323rd BS, 91st Bomb Group (RAF Museum P017523).*

**Below right** *Bassingbourn on 6 June 1944 (US Air Force).*

**Below** *'Yer know how it was?' Captain Chas. E. Cliburn (left), pilot of 'Bad Penny' (124480 of the 322nd Squadron), chats away to Lieutenant James A. Verinis after his 25th mission. Cliburn had been awarded the DFC and the Purple heart (US Air Force).*

in the first raid on Germany when, on 27 January 1943, Wilhelmshaven was raided. A Distinguished Unit Citation was awarded for the attack on Hamm on 3 March 1943 when the weather was bad, the fighting tough. From mid-1943 the targets had become mainly aircraft factories, airfields and oil installations, but deep penetration raids came, to Oranienburg, Peenemünde and Schweinfurt.

Schweinfurt. The very mention of this word at Bassingbourn evoked a silent response, and with good reason. The raid of 17 August 1943 began badly, being delayed whilst the mist cleared. In all some 230 B-17s set off for the distant target, with the 91st leading, Colonel Warzbach at the helm. It was a year to the day since the 8th Air Force had commenced operations in Europe. It was mid-morning when eighteen B-17s formed up over Cambridgeshire, far later than customary. Whey they returned they were within a gaggle of 36 with nine trailing behind, two of which could be seen with engines out of action. They

had, during almost the entire time over enemy territory, been engaged by fighters which concentrated upon the leaders.

During the late evening I recorded in my diary that 'B-17s have come home late'. Little wonder, Schweinfurt for the 91st had been a ghastly experience. At the final count ten of the 36 B-17s lost were from the 91st — and that meant that around a hundred men were missing, many killed in action, in addition to those who reached base seriously wounded. By next morning it was common knowledge locally that the 91st had suffered badly. Indeed, on dispersals at Bassingbourn only three B-17s were to be seen next day, the remainder having been shot down, or presumably taken into hangars for repairs.

Operations were soon resumed and the 91st went again to Schweinfurt, that dreaded place, on 14 October when only one of their eleven aircraft was shot down. There were great names among their Fortresses — 'Jack the Ripper' 41-

**Above** *'What was the party like, then?' Gee, great, just great, Ma.'* Bassingbourn, *December 1944* (US Air Force).

**Below** *B-17F 124504:DF:D, 'The Sad Sack' of the 324th Bomb Squadron on dispersal on 20 March 1944, after its last flight with the Group* (US Air Force).

*24490*, 'Stric Nine' *42-29475*, 'Oklahoma Okie' *42-29921* and, most famous of all, 'Memphis Belle' *41-24485*. To the end of hostilities the 91st was in action, often leading the 8th AF to battle. A few weeks after VE-Day all were gone, a never-to-be forgotten régime of peaches and ice-cream, interminable piles of peanut butter, Dodge trucks, cheery coloured faces and particularly of giant plates of food for incredulous Britishers.

On 26 June 1945 the RAF returned and 47 Group Transport Command took control on 20 July. Nos 422 and 423 Canadian Squadrons arrived but soon disbanded. In August 1945 Liberators of 102 Squadron moved in, mostly in Coastal Command colours. They commenced trooping flights to the Far East in October 1945. No 466 Squadron also arrived in August 1945, disbanding in October. No 102 Squadron moved to Upwood on 15 February 1946 and the following day No 24 (Commonwealth) Squadron and its Dakotas began to arrive from Hendon. Between 16 and 26 February a United Nations delegation attended a radar and radio aids demonstration at Bassingbourn, one of the first airfields to have a Ground Controlled Approach system.

The move of 24 Squadron complete on 25 February, the squadron resumed its role of transporting VIPs, senior officers and government officials concentrating on services conveying up to fourteen passengers in Dakotas between Blackbushe and Prestwick during March 1946. Fourteen VIPs were carried during April, other well-known persons conveyed including Mr Aneurin Bevan carried from Cornwall to Northolt in famous *KP208* on 1 April and Mr Ernest Bevin who on the 28th flew from Le Bourget to Northolt in *KP248*. During May, Field Marshal Smuts journeyed in *KP208* to Gatow from Northolt and Air Chief Marshal Sir John Slessor in *KN386*. Although the aircraft were Bassingbourn-based, they generally picked up their special passengers at Northolt.

No 1359 (VIP) Flight, which arrived from Lyneham in February, was equipped with luxuriously appointed Lancastrians and Yorks and in March 1946 two of the Lancastrians made a record flight to New Zealand. From 3 June, 1359 Flight and 24 Squadron operated as one and on 1 July merged as 24 Squadron whose new Establishment was twelve Dakota 3s and 4s, five Yorks and five Lancastrian IIs. Among the VIP aircraft were Yorks *MW100*, *MW101* and Field Marshal Montgomery's *LV633* containing a huge leather chair for his personal comfort.

It was *MW100* which, after carrying General Sir Arthur Cunningham to Lydda, on 25 July 1946 accomplished a record-breaking 2,660-mile non-stop flight from Habbaniya to Lyneham. Most of the flights were still by Dakota, but on 14 July *MW101* carried Air Vice-Marshal Cochrane on a tour around Mediterranean bases and in August General Alexander was flown overseas in *MW100*. VIPs were still usually flown from Northolt as on 4 August when Lancastrian *VM701* set off carrying Lieutenant General Sir A. C. D. Wiart on a three-and-a-half month tour of China during which it became one of the first aircraft to fly non-stop from Calcutta to Nanking. In China it was joined by *VM727* which between 29 September and 20 December carried Sir Leslie Boyce and a trade mission team. Christmas mail was flown to Australia and New Zealand in York *MW128* and in January 1947 Lord and Lady Mountbatten were flown to Zurich in one of Bassingbourn's Dakotas.

Four Lancastrian crews were chosen to operate a return courier service to Moscow during the 1947 March–April Foreign Ministers' Conference. The aircraft left London at 03:00 GMT and Moscow/Vnukovo at 23:00 GMT every day (except Sunday) between 11 March and 29 April. Other memorable flights that year were to Dorval, Gander and in September–October to Central and South Africa in connection with the Royal Tour. Similar special flights continued

*Bassingbourn, June 1947.*

throughout 1948, although some of the aircraft participated in the Berlin Air Lift flying directly from Bassingbourn to Gatow. There was accordingly a general reduction in VIP flying and indeed activity at Bassingbourn. On 23 March 1946 Oxfords of No 1552 Radio Aids Training Flight had moved in and stayed until 26 October when other Oxfords, this time of 1555 RAT Flight, replaced them on 31 October and remained until 24 March 1947. The training they offered was by now being given by squadrons and not special units.

On 8 June 1949 No 24 Squadron was re-deployed to Waterbeach and was replaced by Yorks of 40, 51 and 59 Squadrons which became effective at their new station on 25 June. Overall control of Bassingbourn now lay with 38 Group, the tactical portion of Transport Command. Nevertheless, the threw new squadrons concentrated each on contributing to the station's five monthly services within Transport Command's schedule trunk network, including flights to Ceylon, Nairobi and sometimes special flights between Manston and Güters-loh or Celle. The 1950 duty, although little changed, was reduced in volume when

No 40 Squadron ceased operations on 20 February and officially disbanded on 15 March. By May a typical month's duty by 51 Squadron resulted in two passenger-cum-freight runs to Nairobi, one passenger and two freight services to Singapore and one special flight. Both 51 and 59 Squadrons disbanded at the end of October 1950, route flying having ceased on 16 October. By 1 November 1950 when Bomber Command repossessed the station, the Bassingbourn scene had changed most unexpectedly. The Korean conflict had brought the Americans back, on 25 August 1950. In April 1944 Bassingbourn's occupants had thrilled to a B-29 Superfortress, the first to visit Britain. Now the 353rd Bomb Squadron, 301st Bomb Group, brought B-29s in plenty.. Dispersals were again full and the Somerset Light Infantry mounted perimeter guard.

The 301st had a prolonged stay due to the international situation. Rotation brought RB-50Bs of the 38th Squadron, 55th Strategic Reconnaissance Wing, in January 1951 and they stayed until May 1951 having undertaken operational flights around the north-west periphery of the USSR. Other January 1951 arrivals were a few B-50Ds of the 341st Bomb Squadron, 97th Bomb Group. This activity had attracted giant C-124A Globemaster IIs, but undoubtedly the most exotic visitor came on 26 April 1951 to remind Bassingbourn of momentous days passed. It was a B-17, *48997*, bringing visitors from the US Embassy. Between May and late August 1951 Bassingbourn was home for the 96th Bomb Squadron, 2nd Bomb Group then on 1 September 1951 the 3913rd Air Base Squadron left for Stansted and remaining Americans deftly departed.

The RAF took over with the arrival of twelve Mosquito T 3s, five PR 34s, two Mosquito VIs, six Meteor T 7s and four PR 10s of 237 OCU. On 1 December 1951 No 231 OCU re-formed, and absorbed them. Then on 13 February 1952 the light bomber training unit, No 204 Advanced

Flying School, arrived from Swinderby — along with Mosquito 3s and 6s. From this was formed 'D' Squadron, 231 OCU, its responsibility the continued training of crews for Mosquito PR squadrons.

To the thrill of all around, in February 1952 came the first Canberra B 2 jet bombers to equip the RAF's No 231 OCU the world's first jet bomber operational training unit. Training using Canberras commenced on 27 May 1952 and by June there were fourteen Canberras at Bassingbourn. A year later the full strength of 26 Canberras was reached and in July 1953 Bassingbourn's first dual-control Canberra T 4 arrived. Seven Canberra PR 3s were received in November 1953 but it was June 1955 before the Meteor PR 10s were retired. Because of the intensity of Canberra bomber crew training, the PR element of 231 OCU was moved first to Merryfield and to Weston Zoyland soon after. It became 237 OCU on 23 October 1956 and was transferred to Wyton in 1958 where on 21 February it disbanded, crews and aircraft moving immediately to become the PR section of 231 OCU at Bassingbourn.

In December 1958 231 OCU was given a wartime operational role. Hardly surprising, for its task put it in the forefront of the introduction of the latest bombing techniques among them LABS, the Low Approach Bombing System using which nuclear stores could be tossed on to a tactical target leaving the aircraft to turn fast and race away. Training for that task commenced at Bassingbourn in 1959, and in April 1960 low-level PR flying was introduced into the syllabus. Originally under 1 Group, 231 OCU was administered by 3 Group between 1 March 1965 and 1 November 1967 then it reverted to 1 Group when No 3 Group disbanded.

A distinguished aeroplane joined 231 OCU on 19 December 1962. This was Canberra PR 3 *WE139* which, flown by Flight Lieutenants R. L. E. Burton and D. H. Cannon, had made the 12,270-mile flight from London to New Zealand in 23

*Canberra B2 WJ728, the author aboard, about to touch down shortly before Bassingbourn's closure* (Alan J. Wright).

hours during the Air Race. The aircraft was at Bassingbourn until April 1969 when it was taken to Henlow. Now it may be seen in the RAF Museum, Hendon.

The visitor to Bassingbourn in June 1967 might hardly have believed his eyes. Six Canberras were painted in Russian markings for a part in the film 'Billion Dollar Brain'. It led to Israeli claims to the effect that the British were colluding with enemies during the Six Day War.

For seventeen years Bassingbourn's Canberras were a very familiar sight in the county's skies, particularly as they turned in near Newmarket on their GCA approaches which led them from one side of the county to the other. By the late 1960s the need for Canberra crews was diminishing and a reduction in training came about. By February 1967, after fifteen years of Canberra flying, 231 OCU had trained over 2,200 pilots and navigators of the RAF, RN and other air forces, and flown some 75 million miles in the course of 163,000 hours of flying. On 19 May 1969 the Canberras taxied out in

force for the last time and in a final show of strength passed in salute over Bassingbourn as they headed for their new base at Cottesmore, and leaving a T 4, *WE195*, to be the last RAF aeroplane to take off from Bassingbourn during the RAF's tenancy.

Apart from one more spell of glory on 27/28 May 1978 when an air display was mounted, Bassingbourn's Air Force days were over. The silence though was once broken when a memorable sound was re-created. It was to Bassingbourn that Glen Miller had brought his music, and almost for the last time. In the hangar he had used, the Syd Lawrence big band re-created the Miller sound, thanks to the East Anglian Aviation Society, on a warm June evening in 1974. The ghosts of the B-17s were very clear and 'Moonlight Serenade' brought back that magic moment when I had climbed aboard 'General Ike' in the same hangar and on the spot where the music was being made.

Now the Queen's Division reigns

*P-47 Thunderbolt poses by a B-17. Claimed to have been taken at Bassingbourn (RAF Museum P100521).*

supreme. Superficially little has really changed, although only a portion of the main runway remains. The saplings which tried to hide the hangars in wartime are now huge trees, and the airfield holds a golf course and entertains land yachts. In the avenue to Rudyard Kipling's Wimpole mansion the elms have all been felled, victims of disease and not intruders of NJG 2 as might have been the case.

The memory of Bassingbourn's flying days has been finely preserved in a museum established by the East Anglian Aviation Society in the original control tower. The latter, of the 1934 twin-box style, was modified in possibly a unique manner in 1942. Being an Army establishment, Bassingbourn is not normally open to visitors. If you wish to visit the tower then contact the Curator, Vince Hemmings, by phoning Letchworth 673340. Contained in the museum are many fascinating exhibits and an excellent photograph collection. The best moments come when one stands on the balcony and imagines a Wimpey trundling by, B-17 combat formations roaring past or Canberras breaking for landing. Gone, all gone.

## Bottisham

*TL540595. S of the A45 about 5 miles E of Cambridge. New A45 road crosses the centre of the airfield*

It was one of those hot, cloudless 1940 days. By chance I took the lane to Wilbraham that used to come off the main Cambridge-Newmarket road. A large expanse of grass followed a wheatfield. No fence, none of the customary barbed wire. Yet on the field, widely dispersed, a clutch of Tiger Moths diverted from their daily flying at Cambridge. Close inspection followed. Incredibly, they had 20 lb bombs hanging from fuselage racks. The situation was indeed alarming. These were attached to Training Command's anti-invasion force, their task to assault enemy troops should they step ashore — and irrespective of losses. Instructors would fly the aircraft.

Bottisham was quickly prepared in May 1940 as a satellite for Waterbeach. It never accepted any aircraft from that station. Instead the Tiger Moths and a few tents for living quarters tarried until September 1940 when the main scare receded, although it was, of course, very late in the war before invasion plans finally elapsed. There was always the fear of raiding parties, if nothing more.

Until the summer of 1941 22 EFTS used Bottisham for Tiger Moth training, then on 15 July 1941 it was taken over by Army Co-operation Command. On to the station came Lysanders of 241 Squadron working closely with Eastern Command Army units and often having detachments at Snailwell.

In August 1941 the sound at Bottisham changed when a few Allison-engined Tomahawks, with their high-pitched rasping sound, supplemented the Lysanders. Their task was fighter-reconnaissance, and they were seen in pairs flying low on training sorties and often 'beating up' Army convoys. Serviceability was poor. There were ground loops and constant engine troubles. No operations were possible.

The next big change occurred on 15 March 1942 when some of the RAF's first Mustang Is arrived for 241 Squadron. Fast and manoeuvrable as it was, the Mustang, whose performance fell off rapidly above 15,000 ft, was a great initial disappointment. These very elegant aircraft quickly became a daily sight in the area. On 2 May 1942 241 Squadron moved to Ayr and 652 Squadron's Tiger Moths, training air observation post pilots, arrived on 15 June, staying here until 21 August when they moved to Westley, near Bury St Edmunds.

Steel net dispersal areas by the A45 side of the field were now protected by earth walls, and a couple of Blister hangars provided for maintenance. A few concrete huts later erected in the northeast corner still stand. On 15 October laying of two metal Sommerfeld track runways commenced, the first coming into use in July 1942.

Newly formed 168 Squadron had flown in from nearby Snailwell on 13 July and again the Tomahawk dominated the scene. Brief excitement came to Bottisham on 23 September when a couple of Whitleys brought in two Horsa gliders, a prelude for things to come. On 7 November eight Mustangs arrived from Ayr for 168 Squadron. Eleven days later five Whitleys and Horsas arrived to transport 168 Squadron to Odiham for operational deployment. After they left, the airfield was placed on Care & Maintenance for major alterations. As a result its two metal runways, '020' of 1,200 yd and '090' of 1,435 yd (and, unusually, 100 yd wide — twice the normal width) were laid and supplemented by a 'T2' hangar, seven Blister hangars, fifteen concrete hardstandings and 68 pierced steel mat dispersals.

On 3 December 1943 the unmistakable din of the Republic P-47 arrived overhead. The 361st Fighter Group, USAAF, was coming and did so in full strength in a matter of days. Operations began on 21 June 1944. Their role was twofold, bomber escort and ground strafing, and they were soon in the thick of the fight. Thus the daily sight now was of P-47s scampering off making an awful racket before forming into their 'finger-four' battle sections.

During May 1944 the 361st began to receive P-51Ds, some of the first in Britain. At the time of D-Day when the Mustangs were dispersed along the airfield perimeter, and the runway now crossed the road where I had enjoyed the site of armed Tiger Moths, some of the P-51s were to be seen with their upper surfaces painted in a superb shade of deep blue. Indeed, that was to become my most vivid memory of the evening of D-Day when I managed a tour of the perimeter, notebook carefully tucked away! Among the Mustangs sat the inevitable Norseman and Bobcat.

Bottisham's Mustangs were extremely

**Above** *Bottisham was home for P-51s of the 361st Fighter Group* (US Air Force).

**Below** *Ground crew watch a P-51 landing at Bottisham on 7 June 1944* (US Air Force).

*'Lou IV', a P-51D* 413410 *based at Bottisham in 1944* (RAF Museum P017503).

busy during that summer, operating mainly over France. As soon as the A-20 Group left Little Walden in September the 361st moved there, for it was a far better-equipped station. Bottisham then lay silent.

In 1945 some Belgian airmen training at Snailwell were billeted at Bottisham, their Tiger Moths visiting the airfield. Bottisham, closed on 1 May 1946, was sold on 1 October 1958.

On a blustery afternoon, 14 February 1948, I happened to be passing as bulldozers went into action. A few minutes later the control tower was mere rubble. Gateposts for the main entrance on the old A45 remain, white of course, and dual carriageway travellers nearby race across peacetime fields once used for war, understandably unaware of its all but hidden past.

## Bourn

*TL340590. On A45 7 miles W of Cambridge*
No surviving record indicates when Bourn first resounded to an aircraft arriving, but Wellingtons of 101 Squadron and Stirlings of No 7 certainly used the landing ground from spring 1941, for this was Oakington's satellite. The enemy also put in an early appearance, a Ju 88C intruder attacking on 9 April and placing three bombs on to a runway. Two Stirlings homed to Bourn on return from the memorable daylight raid on Brest on 18 December 1941, the battered form of one sitting at the end of the main runway throughout Christmas 1941.

Relieving pressure on the parent station, No 101 Squadron arrived from Oakington on 11 February 1942 with its newly received Wellington IIIs. After operating veteran Mk Ic *R1780* 'B-Beer' against Le Havre on 13 March and Lille on the 16th — the aircraft then having completed 35 sorties before moving to 11 OTU, Bassingbourn — a month's conversion to Mk IIIs followed. Their first use came against Cologne on 13 March. Although 500 and 1,000 lb HE bombs were carried, the Wellingtons usually

*XV Squadron Stirling III LS:V-BK652 and Mk 1 LS:S-R9193 distant at Bourn in 1943* (RAF Museum P10214).

delivered bundled flares and frequently nine SBCs each containing 80 × 4 lb incendiaries. Such fire raisers were showered upon Lübeck on 28 March, and on Rostock on both 23 and 25 April during major raids. Twelve 101 Squadron crews participated in the Cologne '1,000 bomber' raid, two failing to return. From Bourn another five Wellingtons also operated, a detachment of 23 OTU Pershore, and these also took part in the Essen '1,000 Plan' raid of 1 June when 101 Squadron despatched ten aircraft. Against Bremen on 25 June sixteen Wellingtons of 101 Squadron were fielded, and when on 11 August 1942 the move to Stradishall commenced the squadron had from Bourn mounted sixty operations, flown 461 sorties, seven times taken part in minelaying and lost seven aircraft during operations. Prior to mining sorties the Wellingtons would each be seen taking aboard two 1,500 lb green-painted tubular mines quite unlike any bombs in appearance.

The Wellingtons moved when the Pathfinder Force (8 Group) took over Wyton as its headquarters station and nudged XV Squadron's Stirlings to Bourn. The first of their 104 operations and 615 sorties from Bourn was a raid against Düsseldorf in August. The Stirlings took part in the autumn long-distance harrowing night raids on northern Italy, the aircrafts' poor altitude performance forcing some outward flights by the heavily loaded bombers to be made between alpine peaks. At the end of 1942 XV Squadron commenced trials with the first of the refined Stirling IIIs, operating the new variant for the first time on 7 February 1943. It was disappointing and Stirling losses remained high, XV Squadron losing 26 aircraft during operations from Bourn.

Just as the 1943 bombing offensive became really underway, XV Squadron was ordered to Mildenhall. After attacking Frankfurt on 10 April the squadron commenced its move, partly travelling in style with the aid of Horsa gliders. In its place came No 97 (Straits Settlement)

Squadron, a 5 Group formation on loan to the Pathfinders to increase their strength and perform in a 'back-up' flare dropping/marker force. The newcomers arrived on 18 April and first operated, against Duisburg, on 26 April. During May a third Flight was added, and the squadron bombed distant Pilsen on 13/14 May and took part in heavy raids on Wüppertal and Essen. A special raid was mounted by four crews flying from Scampton on 16 June who bombed Friedrichshafen, flew on to Maison Blanche in a shuttle operation, and attacked La Spezia on return.

The Straits Settlement Squadron, 97, played a marker role in the huge Hamburg raids, sent sixteen aircraft to Peenemünde and then entered the Battle of Berlin. *EE105* 'Q Queenie', returning from the 'Big City' on 23 August, was shot down by an intruder over Norfolk. There were hosts of eventful moments for the Lancaster crews on every raid and particularly during the seventeen attacks on Berlin in which they had participated from Bourn by the end of 1943.

One night came to be outstanding. Twenty-one Lancasters set off for Berlin on 16 December 1943 and the opposition was strong. But it was the return to Bourn which proved quite disastrous, for bad visibility set in over the area and 28 aircrew were killed as aircraft short of fuel crashed. Eight crews landed safely at Bourn, three at Graveley. Flight Sergeant Coates had incendiaries from another aircraft fall on his, and flak put two engines out of action. He thought he would have to ditch, but managed to bring the crippled Lancaster into Downham. Two Lancasters crashed near Ely and Wyton and another was lost without trace. Flying Officer Thackway crashed near Bourn, two more crashed near Graveley and one near Gransden. Another, flown by Squadron Leader Mackenzie, could be seen next morning as a burnt wreck by the side of the main road. The night's disaster was the worst suffered by any East Anglian airfield in such circumstances.

The squadron noticeably operated with great efficiency and intensively, delivering many 4,000 pound 'cookies' as well as marker loads. On 18 March 1944 'C' Flight was detached to Downham Market to form the nucleus of 635 Squadron. By that time the squadron had added Schweinfurt to its 'targets attacked' list, and raided Augsburg again. For '97' that held bitter memories of its costly daylight venture in April 1942. Bombing emphasis was about to switch to transport facilities in France and Belgium when the last Lancaster sortie touched down after attacking Aachen on 11/12 April 1944. Bourn's Lancasters had flown 1,158 sorties during 92 operations which resulted in the loss of 49 Lancasters. At midday on 18 April 1944, 21 Lancasters left for Coningsby where 5 Group welcomed back one of the 'crack' bomber squadrons.

Runway building was about to commence at Marham, so in the late morning of 23 March 1944, No 105 Mosquito Squadron roared glamorously into Bourn. This was a squadron with a glittering war record, the premier Mosquito day bomber squadron. Some of the glamour of those days had been lost when they were switched to night bombing, but now *Oboe*-equipped and flying Mk IXs, they were to hold as important a place at night as any squadron. On the evening of the day of their arrival they operated marking Laon's marshalling yards. Next night they marked airfields during a Berlin raid, for the range of *Oboe* was limited. Their main task at this time was marking transport targets in occupied countries and airfields, then they placed their target indicators on gun batteries along the French coast, and spearheaded bomber attacks in a prelude to the Normandy landings.

Next came a busy period when they operated by day and night against V-1 targets before finding oil refineries. By now they had some Mosquito XVIs with cabin pressurization. Their Mosquitoes carried out bombing raids in their own right too, and were able to place their

*Most celebrated of all Mosquitoes, Bourn's Mk IX* GB:F-LR503 *photographed after the 203rd of its record 213 operational sorties.*

loads with enviable accuracy. Things did not go all their own way though for, as they returned from Orleans and Le Mans on 23 May, an intruder bombed and strafed Bourn, damaging two aircraft on the ground and holding up landing by an hour.

By late 1944 the Mosquitoes' operational effective range was extended by modified *Oboe*, and continental stations permitted *Oboe* operations from Bourn deeper into enemy territory. They marked, too, for the Late Night Striking Force, whose sting was as great as many a Main Force raid and often more accurate.

On 18 December 1944 a new squadron, No 162, formed at Bourn with Canadian-built Mosquito XXs and XXVs. A proportion of its aircraft were equipped with $H_2S$ and they, too, adopted partly a marker role. They could mark for their own crews and soon began the nightly —

even twice nightly — run to Berlin. What was even more important, these raids were almost without loss, and with accurate and heavy loads. Bourn was indeed a busy station, equipped with the most cost-effective warplane of all time.

A new shape came to Bourn in March 1945 when Spitfire Vs and Hurricane IIs of 1686 Bomber Defence Training Flight used the station giving training for 8 Group crews in fighter defence. Stirlings were part of Bourn from 1941 to the end of the war. From the Sebro factory on Madingley Road, Cambridge, the bombers or transports were brought to Bourn, erected in the 'T' hangars still to be seen on the eastern side of the airfield, and test-flown from the airfield.

By August 1945 the scene had changed. No 105 Squadron left in June 1945 and 162 moved to Blackbushe on 10 July to fly mail and courier flights to distant parts of Europe. Sebro began

overhauling Transport Command Liberators, work continuing almost to the end of that year.

On 1 January 1946 3 Group handed the station to 48 Group and on 21 July 1947 it passed to Maintenance Command. It closed in 1948 and the land was sold in April 1961.

Bourn had lain dormant until Pest Control moved in to offer helicopter spraying services from the north-eastern corner of the airfield. Management Aviation followed them many years later and this concern also carried out crop spraying using helicopters. Rotorcraft has an overhaul hangar here, and in 1985 Bond Helicopters took over the Management Aviation site. Much of wartime RAF Bourn has long since gone, but on the southern side of the airfield, where once 105 Squadron dispersed, private flying takes place. Among the tenants is the RFC — the Rural Flying Corps — which operates a Percival Provost and an even rarer bird, a Percival Sea Prince.

## Cambridge

*TL487586. By Newmarket Road, at the eastern boundary of Cambridge*
From 'Tiger' to TriStar, a colossal leap by any reckoning and accomplished uniquely by Marshall of Cambridge! Since 26 January 1938, when *K4249* and *K4270*, Cambridge's first two Tiger Moths, moved in, some of those de Havilland biplanes have been in residence, which may constitute a record. On few days, within that time too, has a Gipsy engine not been heard purring its way around the Cambridge circuit.

In 1983 the scene spectacularly changed when the first gigantic Lockheed TriStar touched down to dwarf not only the Tiger Moths but even their homes. Most unusual of all one may with luck, and only at Cambridge, find a Tiger Moth of the 1930s, *G-AOEI* once *N6946* and which served in France with 81 Squadron in 1939–40, trotting by an example of the RAF's biggest aeroplane of all time, the TriStar. You may even sense it whisper 'I've made it for nearly fifty years — beat that!' It might also be muttering in superior tones 'I knew your cousins long removed. I was at Llandow when Sir Arthur used to send his Albemarles and Whitleys there during the war. What is more, I was once a part, a small part, of the Top Peoples' private 'airline', No 24 Squadron when I was stationed at Hendon from October 1940 until late 1942. I even knew King George!'

For over three-quarters of a century Marshall has been a familiar Cambridge name. During that period the family bus-

iness has handled a wide variety of road vehicles and been a major agency for Austin, Morris and latterly British Leyland. Great effort has been expended in making the company a success. Its origin stems from Mr D. G. Marshall's interest in early cars around the time of the 1914-18 war. Since 1929 the name 'Marshall' has, in Cambridgeshire, been synonymous with aviation and the firm is now headed by Sir Arthur Marshall, the son of its founder.

The first Cambridge aerodrome, which came into use in April 1929, occupied a site immediately eastwards of where the Newmarket Road Cambridge United Football Club ground stands. Almost nothing is left of the original airfield which officially opened to the accompaniment of an air display on 9 June 1929. The

**Right** *Three pioneers! From left Mr D.G. Marshall, Alan Cobham and Mr A.G. Marshall, the present Sir Arthur Marshall (Marshall Engineering).*

**Above** *ZD953 about to leave to become the RAF's first TriStar tanker.*

**Above left** *Don't forget the Tigers, Sir! And who, surely, ever would?*

*DH 60s and a visiting Westland Wessex (old type) at the first Cambridge Airport (Marshall Engineering).*

rough lane which led to the site remains along with a tree from those times, but most of the one-time aerodrome where private flying training began in October 1929 lies beneath Whitehill Estate. Apart from the Cambridge Aero Club, founded in November 1934, and the University Aero Club, formed in April 1936, the aerodrome hosted an air taxi element and had many interesting visitors. If the land could talk it would tell of the late Sir Alan Cobham's Circus with its Avro 504s, Airspeed Ferry and a host of well-known people who flew there. It would surely recall the smart 1935 General Aircraft Jubilee Monospar, Cierva C 30A autogiros and one of 19-Squadron's early Gauntlets here for a Saturday afternoon display.

Active always were Marshalls' DH 60Gs, *G-AAEH* registered to Mr A. G. G. Marshall on 8 February 1929 and which joined the Cambridge Aero Club on 13 November 1934, and *G-EBYZ*, the first production example. Flown by W.L Hope,

the latter won the 1928 King's Cup Air Race at an average speed of 105 mph. *G-EBYZ* was destroyed in a crash near Hauxton on 20 September 1932.

Cambridge was a turning point for the September 1937 King's Cup Air Race which had eyes scanning in for a fleeting view of the DH TK 4, Edgar Percival in his Mew Gull and Ken Waller's DH 88 Comet Racer. The aerodrome might, just, smile at the thought of a little curly haired boy bravely truanting from school to enjoy a glimpse of Henri Mignet and his Flying Flea on a rough and rainy afternoon. Possibly it chuckled that day when the little boy's uncle greeted him saying 'Well, Michael, I AM surprised to see you'.

Most of all the old field would surely look back in joy to the silver and black Gipsy Moths which chugged in over the housetops of Newmarket Road in a manner unacceptable in the modern world. Well, of course, flying really was flying then and people were more sensibly tolerant.

There was, though, no question about one thing, the airfield was far too small to have much future. Knowing of the Air Ministry's desire for a reserve training centre at Cambridge, Marshall in 1935 acquired a large area of land on the Cambridge boundary and spreading into the Parish of Teversham. It took two years to convert the fields into an aerodrome extensive and very modern by the standards of those days. A smart 'No 1 Hangar' was flanked by a dope shop and an impressive office, club house and control centre with a commanding position for viewing all that was to take place. The Airport Hotel was to become a popular refuelling spot, while further away was spacious No 2 Hangar not completed until spring 1939 and from which 22 Elementary & Reserve Flying Training School would function. Before the latter officially opened on 1 February 1938 and training began, the school had received two brand new Hawker Hart (T)s, *K6451* on 21 January and *K6465* on 27 January as well as the two Tiger Moths. Flying from the new aerodrome had been commenced by the DH 60s and others of Marshall's Flying School in September 1937.

Saturday, 8 October 1938, witnessed the grand ceremonial opening display, the profits from which, let it be well noted, were given to Addenbrooke's Hospital. Silver-painted DH 86B *L7596* of 24 Squadron brought in Sir Kingsley Wood and his entourage and as he concluded his speech three half-camouflaged Hart species roared off in approval. By this time 22 E&RFTS had acquired two Audaxes and held six 'Tigers'. Parked on the north-eastern area of the flying ground near to where 'the mound' now is were about fifty visiting aircraft. What a fabulous sight they would now present, what masses would swoon! For the flying show the Dutch contributed a 'Scheldemusch', a curious contraption which its designer claimed could never crash. An all-white Monospar Ambulance appeared, nine Avro Tutors of the CUAS

flew around, Reggie Brie gyrated in a Cierva C 30 and Captain Edgar Percival displayed a Mew Gull and his very elegant pale blue Q 6 twin-engined airliner which looked lovely as it hurried around very low. But there was no doubting the stars despite their camouflage.

Outside the terminal building they paraded in line, three of 19 Squadron's super Spitfires. When they flew, led by Squadron Leader H. I. Cozens, they did so to great adulation from the moderate sized crowd and the loudspeakers' cry 'fastest aeroplanes in the world'. Barely had they taxied in when sightseers mobbed them. A media man grabbed me, planted me by a Spitfire, said smile, then shot me. Moments later we were both in the unfriendly arms of a giant threatening 'bobby'. It really was a splendid afternoon, and for me the start of a lifetime's excitement for so much has happened at Cambridge to thrill any aviation enthusiast.

On 1 February 1939 50 Group seized control of 22 E&RFTS and soon started the Direct Entry RAF Officer's Course here where eight civilian instructors handled 32 pupils. Weekend flying by the 'VR' involved five Harts, two Audaxes, four Hinds, the Tiger Moths and five Fairey Battles — the first of which, *K7618* and *K7625*, arrived on 20 December 1938 — generated much public interest, and 22 E&RFTS was to prove by far the best operated of all of these schools.

The civilians, too, made their mark and especially in May 1939 when the first of two DH 94 Moth Minors, *G-AFNG* and *G-AFNJ*, joined the Marshall team training under the Civil Air Guard Scheme. In 1939 that included four DH 60Gs, *G-AAEH*, *G-AAVY*, *G-ABDU* and *G-ABOY*. More unusual were Marshall's Flying School's four DH 60M Moths — *G-AACD*, the pre-production demonstration example, *G-AACU* which Marshall acquired from the famous de Havilland School of Flying at Stag Lane, *G-AASR* and *G-ABPJ*, which began life as *EI-AAE* of the Irish Aero Club before becoming

**Top** *'19's Spitfires, opening day October 1938. K9795 nearest fought in the Battle of Britain with Nos 64, 603 Squadrons. Centre, K9789, the first squadron Spitfire, was with 65 Squadron in 1940* (Marshall Engineering).

**Above** *Spring 1939, at the new airport. DH 60s nearest, RAF Tiger Moths camouflaged, harts and distantly two Battles. The buildings have not changed much since then* (Marshall Engineering).

**Below** *Pre-war Moth Minor, G-AFNG, still going strong as a Coupé.*

*G-ABPJ* in August 1931. The DH 60M had a metal frame fuselage suiting it particularly for use overseas. Puss Moth *G-ABIZ* was replaced in July 1938 by DH Leopard Moth *G-ACRV*. Flying instruction on the Moths cost £1 10/- an hour, £2 on the Puss Moth.

By September 1939 200 VR pilots had commenced training, seventy had their 'wings', 95 had flown at night and 52 been solo on a Battle. To give the VR pilots a taste of flying in modern aeroplanes there were visits by Tiger-engined Whitley IIIs of 7 Squadron which parked themselves alongside the low hedge by Teversham Lane. In those days people were so well behaved that there was no fence there, just the hawthorn which nobody would have ever dreamed of finding a way through. As well as the Whitleys there was the mobile Chance light to help with night flying, and the 'Cambridge Roller' to watch, a massive array of lengthy rollers spread behind a tractor which could flatten considerable areas of land at a blow and cut grass too. Mowing a large airfield still brings problems and is costly.

With little ceremony and probably no particular welcome the Tiger Moths slotted in neatly alongside the DH 60Gs. From 1938 to 1951 'Tigers' much frequented the local sky. At one time there were nearly 180 based here for the 240 pupils, and it was quite normal to see as many as thirty exploring the circuit at one time. 'Marshall's Messerschmitts' people came to irreverently call them. Among their pupils were many who would soon achieve fame, including 'Johnnie' Johnson, the RAF's top scoring fighter pilot.

All the civilian aircraft were grounded as soon as war commenced and later impressed for military service. The Hart variants also left and 24 instructors from Ipswich and Oxford arrived, also more Tiger Moths. On 6 November 1939 the first wartime eight-week course commenced, by which time Marshall had taken on a very new task, as Civilian Repair Organization responsible for looking after the wooden Airspeed Oxford trainer and the metal Whitley bomber. Whitleys came in hundreds and Oxfords were dealt with to the end of the war. Each one left in superb condition for high quality workmanship has always been the firm's hall mark.

On 1 January 1940 all the instructors

*Puss Moth* G-ABIZ *at the first Cambridge aerodrome* (Marshall Engineering).

were drafted into the RAF as part of No 22 Elementary Flying Training School which title the unit acquired in September 1939. During May 1940, with the war taking an alarming turn, the pupil population rose from 96 to 104, course length was cut to seven weeks and the Tiger Moths were placed in two Flights, one of twenty and one of forty aircraft. So desperate was the need for pilots that the course length was cut to six weeks (44 hours) in June when Cambridge became an operational RAF station.

It was in mid-June that the first Lysanders arrived, to disperse on the southern and eastern sides of the airfield. They belonged to No 2 Squadron (identity letters *KO*) whose Lysander IIs were attached to XI Army Corps until late January 1941. With their arrival came the closure of Teversham Lane, and Newmarket Road between the aerodrome gate and the Lane. On 29 June fifteen more Lysanders, over half of them veterans of the French campaign and this time of 16 Squadron (identity letters *UG*) arrived from Redhill and stayed until it

moved to Okehampton at the start of August. The Lysander squadrons from 1 July daily mounted two-aircraft patrols at dawn and again at dusk along the coastline between the Nene mouth and Wells-next-Sea and from there to Lowestoft, watching for any signs of a German invasion. By the time of its move No 16 Squadron alone had flown 104 searching sorties between Wells and Lowestoft. 'B' Flight of 26 Squadron arrived on 3 August replacing 16 Squadron, and like its companion received training in the use of 250 lb gas bombs in case the enemy contravened the Geneva Convention. Brief trials of the Defiant turret fighter were undertaken by 2 Squadron to assess its suitability for ground strafing, and in the autumn a few 20 mm cannon became available for attachment to the Lysander stub wings.

Meanwhile 22 EFTS had been given an operational role within Plan 'Banquet Light' under which two Flights each of five Tiger Moths piloted by instructors were in July attached to 2 Corps. Each Tiger Moth was fitted with bomb racks to

*Lysander II KO:Q of 2 Squadron flying near Cambridge, September 1940* (W. Shearman, via A.S. Thomas).

carry 8 × 20 lb fragmentation F bombs which were to be aimed in dives of up to 60 degrees down to 650 ft, then the aircraft would rely upon low flying and good manoeuvrability for escape. This was a commitment which lasted certainly into 1942 with 22 EFTS being attached to 268 Squadron at Bury in September 1940 and from April 1941 at Snailwell. By August 1941 five Flights of Tiger Moths (there were seventy Flights in all) were trained for 'Banquet' and then attached to the 6th Armoured Division via 241 Squadron, Bottisham. Since July 1940 the latter had served as a Relief Landing Ground for 22 EFTS. An increased number of aircraft at Cambridge resulted from the formation of No 4 (Supplementary) Flying Instructors' School (known from 13 January 1942 as No 4 FIS and here until late 1942).

August 1940 found Marshall also repairing Hart variants. Additional and dispersed premises for such work were necessary and found close by, notably at Nightingale's Garage near River Lane, premises which remained in use almost to the end of the war. Already the enemy had bombed the area and the afternoon of 26 August brought an alert during which a half-yellow Heyford bomber circled and landed for a few days' stay. The enemy was probably more interested in other things when early on 3 September 1940 a Heinkel He 111 dropped the first bombs on the aerodrome, three HEs and a few incendiaries which fell near Lysanders in the south-west corner. It was at about this time that another RLG, at Caxton Gibbet, came in use for night flying. To improve vehicle travel around the aerodrome a cement perimeter track on the east and south sides was authorized.

On 18 September 1940 239 Squadron re-formed and almost at once the six Lysanders of its 'B' Flight were attached to the 2nd Armoured Division and posted to Cambridge, staying until 22 January 1941. At the end of September 268 Squadron formed at Bury and placed ten ex-2 Squadron KO-marked Lysanders at Cambridge for three weeks' work-up.

No confirmation has ever come to the

*Defiant* KO:I-N1572 *of 2 Squadron at Cambridge for ground strafing trials in August 1940* (W. Shearman, via Andrew Thomas).

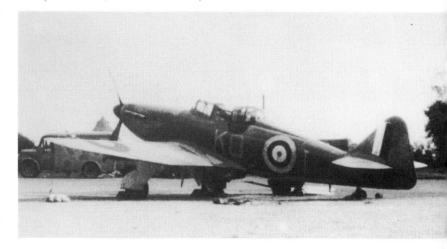

story that on 28 October a ferry pilot coming to collect an Oxford did so in a Percival Mew Gull. He is said to have circled the airfield and then dived upon it, crashing the unusual aeroplane into the ground. He is said to have survived, the wreckage being taken into a hangar. Remnants of two Mew Gulls were written off at Luton in July 1945, perhaps including those remains? The story is far from confirmed.

Throughout 1940 Oxfords and Whitleys processed through the works which, along with the EFTS, attracted many important visitors. One such was the Chief of Staff, Royal Canadian Air Force. His visit took place on 30 December, and soon he had a visitor — most unwelcome too. After visiting Waterbeach a Dornier Do 215 (unusual sight at any time) circled south-east of Cambridge and then made several passes over a period of twenty minutes and put bullets into three Tigers, an Oxford, Magister and a 'Lyssie'. The 1,300 rounds fired from a Lewis gun had no effect upon the intruder and morale was not increased when a Spitfire passed by 'on the other side.'. As a cartridge case whizzed by me to ram into the roof of the Brunswick School a knowall alongside assured me the pilot had 'been up at the University'. The thought occurred to me that maybe he'd been at the school too and did not enjoy the experience!

Four HE bombs which fell at Cherry Hinton on 9 May 1941 were probably intended for Marshall's. The acute scare over invasion had by then subsided so on 24 May the roads by the aerodrome were opened for daylight transit. As I made the welcome journey I noted on the field 56 Tiger Moths, five Hinds, three Magisters of 4 (S) FIS and two Whitley Vs. Another two dozen Tiger Moths were at Bottisham.

At 03:15 hrs on 9/10 September 1941 a low-flying Ju 88C of NJG 2 roared in from the north-west and hurled nine HEs at the airfield. Thanks to an overshoot the only damage was superficial, to several Oxfords, in what was a potentially damaging strike. Such intruder raids were about to cease and that permitted, on 25 November 1941, the first night flying of the war from Cambridge. It was an interesting event for six trainees were soon to be experimentally trained here, entirely in darkness. Next night a passing Ju 88 promptly brought a cry for 'lights out!'

The procession of visiting aircraft throughout the war reads like an aircraft recognition handbook. Great excitement came on 11 December 1941 when a Hector released a Hotspur 1. The first of hosts of Fairchild Argus 1 ATA transports called on 13 February 1942. On 22 February a Mosquito made the type's first visit and later that day Walrus *AQ:L* of 276 Squadron came for tea. The first Beaufort to visit did so on 5 July, and on 1 August a Whitley/Horsa trainer (*DP370*) combination made three releases/take-offs in a most impressive demonstration.

The Instructors' School had received a boost when in May 1942 it received a few Master Is which shortly after had their wing tips clipped. When taking off the Rolls-Royce Kestrel-engined machines sounded like Hurricanes and nothing like the Harts of yesteryear. To distinguish No 4 FIS from 22 EFTS (whose aircraft carried identity numbers between *1* and *150*) its Tiger Moths on their cowlings carried *AA,BB,CC*, etc, the Magisters *A1,A2,A3*, etc, and the Masters *AB,BC,CD*, etc, the fifth and final example joining during August 1942, by which time an entirely new shape was on the premises.

Even before it flew the Armstrong-Whitworth Albemarle was a well-known shape for, incredibly, official silhouettes depicting the aircraft were within any self-respecting aviation enthusiast's 1940 collection! Problem was, they were never matched with a sighting. For me that came on 6 July 1942, the date upon which parts of an Albemarle arrived on a 'sixty-footer' at Marshall's and were hidden behind the most northerly hangar on

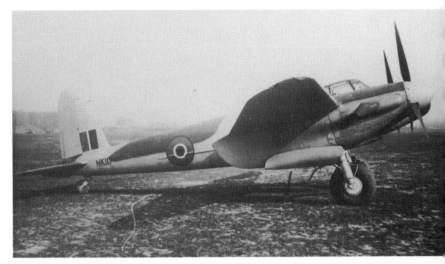

*Mosquito* HK117 *at Cambridge in March 1943, after conversion to Mk XII.*

the north site and thus easily viewed from the Borough Cemetery. It was December 1942 when an Albemarle first flew from Cambridge, and these shapely aeroplanes gradually came for overhaul and modification in increasing numbers, eventually replacing Whitleys.

Interesting as they were the Albemarles were quite eclipsed when on 4 February 1943 two Mosquito NF IIs raced into the circuit and peeled away fighter-style into a grand partnership. They had come to receive centimetric radar and became Mk XIIs. Later arrivals were fitted with American radar and changed into Mk XVIIs.

Around February 1943 there was another rare sight at Cambridge for several ageing Fortress Is came for overhaul, which attracted a visit by a Coastal Command Fortress II on 28 March to allow pilot training. The old Fortresses had emerged from the paint shop in the latest white scheme of Coastal Command with whom they were to serve as operational trainers. Getting them airborne from a relatively short run was

looked upon with deep feelings, and to do so one revved up close to the stop butts by Newmarket Road, then roared away tremendously — and skimmed over the southern boundary hedge to the delight of peeping Mikes! Maybe the old Fort thought its eye sight was failing when on 19 February it must have noticed the arrival of the twin-tailed Oxford.

Being much a part of Cambridge this major local employer participated in local wartime fund raising events, In May 1943 Tiger Moth *N6971: 140* sat in the Corn Exchange making money in Wings for Victory Week, and three Master Is paraded over the town. On the 13th even more amazing was the passage of a host of 39 Tiger Moths staggering in the wind! Is that the largest such swarm?

Precious moments ever multiplied as on 29 May when a Firefly I prototype did some local flying. A few days later Auster AOP Is in trainer trim started arriving and 22 EFTS commenced initial training of Army pilots selected to fly air observation post Austers.

There was no mistaking the next regular Marshall customer, whose raucous din rent the air. This was the Hawker Typhoon, several hundred of which came for repair, overhaul or modification. The first to be cleared was *JR209* which arrived in March 1944. Fitting air cleaners to Typhoon radiators was one essential task undertaken.

For a week in March 1944 a small casualty clearing section, No 92 Staging Post, established itself in the north-east corner of the airfield, during a 46 Group exercise for its ambulance role in the invasion. This attracted a famous veteran, Harrow *K6993* now *BJ:L* of 271 Squadron and which in 1940 was involved in aerial minelaying over the south coast. Carrying stretchers, it later served in France and Belgium only to be destroyed in Operation 'Bodenplatz' when fighter-bombers assaulted 2 TAF on New Year's Day 1945. With it, and more portentous, came the first Dakota to touch down at Cambridge, *FZ685*. By late summer 1944 Marshall was overhauling Dakotas as well as Typhoons and Albemarles — still an important part of

the RAF's transport force. They supplanted Whitleys here and in the transport and glider tug role. The last Whitley, *EB302*, left Cambridge in May 1944 although Whitley remains, including Coastal Command GR VIIs, long survived.

Early 1945 found Marshall handling black Mosquito IIs of 100 Group, and Mk XIIIs. Late production Albemarles were around, the first Mk VI to fly after modification doing so on 7 April. By then the airfield had all but received its first indicatioin of post-war work. On 2 March a large-scale 38 Group exercise for the Rhine crossing was routed over Cambridge. As Halifax *9U:D* passed over, its tow rope departed from Hamilcar *NX816* which abruptly turned to make a force landing and in the process undershot the aerodrome.

In August *TK745*, the first of an intended 75 Hamilcars to be fitted with two Pegasus engines enabling them to assist in being towed to the Far East, arrived for modification. The plan was cancelled before work started and the

*Sounding like an overgrown Anson, Herr Himmler's personal Fw 200C-4 (0137) Condor* GC+AE *called at Marshall's on 7 July 1945* (RAE).

110 ft span glider was taken apart, like a clutch of rare Spitfire PR Xs placed in a graveyard established by Meadowlands.

By the end of the war Marshall had trained over 20,000 pilots at Cambridge and its other EFTS, No 29, at Clyffe Pypard. Without doubt 22 EFTS was the most productive flying school. The CRO had handled over 5,000 aircraft at Cambridge while working parties operated far from home. After the war work continued on Mosquitoes and Dakotas, then came another milestone. On 1 January 1946 an aged Tiger Moth, G-ACDG flown by Lady Bragg, made the first post-war private civil flight in Britain. Marshall's soon had a couple of Rapides, one of which — G-AHED — is now in the hands of the RAF Museum.

The EFTS, which by 1945 comprised five Flights, was gradually reduced, and closed on 30 April 1947. Its replacement was No 22 Reserve Flying School which also flew Tiger Moths and which re-equipped with Chipmunks in 1951 and disbanded on 30 April 1954. The RFS had followed in the footsteps of the Cam-bridge University Air Squadron which re-opened here in 1944 and used Tiger Moths, including the wartime impressed quiet one, W7950 ex-G-AFSL and Cirrus-powered. In January 1950 the CUAS became the second unit to fly Chipmunks. It now flies Bulldogs, the first of which was received in March 1975.

Little known is it that on 14 September 1946 'Marshall's' was open for a Battle of Britain Day display. Items for viewing included York KY:AW and Lancaster TW893-KO:F of 115 Squadron which horrifically ploughed through a flock of plovers as it landed. A Meteor III flew around, but not until 19 March 1947, did a jet, Meteor EE 409-DL:F of 92 Squadron, land at Cambridge, when short of fuel.

Like so many civil operators, Marshall's acquired an Autocrat, G-AHAW, and a rare immediate post-war visitor was often the Spitfire G-AHZI owned by Mr Bramson. One of the rarest and oldest aircraft ever to touch down here since the war was a Klemm KI 25a coupé, HB-ETU, from Switzerland on 4 May 1947, advertising holidays in Arosa.

*RAF Tiger Moths, like DE998 of 22 RFS, flew from Cambridge for fourteen years* (D.C.V. Simmonds).

**Above** *Regular 1946 Sunday visitor. Resting alongside part of Marshall's vehicle industry and No 1 hangar, Mr Spiller's still active Miles M38 G-AKIN.*

**Above right** *Chipmunks have been busy at Cambridge since 1950. Familiar Anson VV312 pokes its rear into view, outside No 2 Hangar.*

**Right** *Cambridge's first jet visitor, Meteor III EE409 of 92 Squadron* (Alan J. Wright).

**Below right** *The first civilian Spitfire, Mk 11b G-AHZI, prepared by Marshall at Cambridge* (Marshall Engineering).

**Below** *Exotic visitor on 25 September 1947, Hawker Tomtit G-ABII. The distant Blister hangar and near buildings remain.*

48

As re-armament picked up in the 1950s Marshall's maintained RAF Dakotas for the Berlin Airlift and modified Mosquito 35s into target towers. Then came Sea Hornets, which programme slipped into refurbishing and modifying Venom NF 2s whose fins needed changing, and the completion of Venom fighter-bombers. After the war Marshall's drawing office and design department expanded, early endeavours surrounding ideas for a small feeder liner. Assisting in the vital expansion of the RAF's all-weather fighter force, Marshall had the task of converting Brigands into T 4 and 5 radar trainers, and of fitting AI Mk 17 (destined for the Javelin 1) into the Valetta T 4. Boundary layer research (with possible application to naval fighters) was undertaken at Cambridge, first with an Anson and later with *VF665*, the ill-fated MA 4.

In the mid-1950s came that outstanding post-war aeroplane the Canberra, large numbers of which have passed through the works. For these heavier jet aircraft a runway was essential and Marshall had a long concrete one laid. It was strong enough to allow work to be undertaken on many Valiant V-bombers. Britannias came for overhaul, fitting out or storage, likewise Airspeed Ambassasor and Comet airliners. Franchises were awarded for the overhaul of Gulfstream

**Right** *Gone for ever — dear old Teversham Lane, as an Indian Viscount lands.*

**Below right** *Rapides including* G–AGZO *were much a part of post-war Marshall activity.*

**Below** *Cambridge not long after the war* (Marshall Engineering).

*RAF 'Hercs' arrived from America unpainted, like* XV197.

prop jets, and extended in recent years to rich man's joy, the magnificent Gulfstream 2 and 3. Similar work is linked to the Cessna Citation business jet for a wide range of customers, civilian and military. Boeing 727s also come for attention, and soon possibly 747s.

In the early 1960s the flying school began to operate Cessna 150s in place or worthy Tigers. De Havilland Rapides were replaced by a Piper Apache and then a Beech Queenair. Currently a Citation acts as the company's commuter.

An exacting time came when Marshall acquired work on Concorde, an accolade for any aviation concern. Noses were built to amazingly precise measurements on a specially levelled pad in No 2 Hangar. Using a very modern tape-controlled milling machine, side panels were also produced for Concorde engine nacelles. Design work was undertaken in connection with fighter weapons and the

Saro F 177 rocket fighter. A Vulcan called for modifications to allow it to carry an RB 199 engine in connection with Tornado development for which two Buccaneers also called for instrumentation.

The 19th of December 1966 proved to be a very special day in Cambridge's history for it witnessed the arrival of *XV177*, the first of hosts of Lockheed Hercules transports. Marshall had secured a contract to look after the type in RAF service and paint them in a strange two-tone brown and black scheme. That was a specialized task, Marshall pioneering use of polyurethane initially on a Vampire T 11. Painting was done in a new, large hangar where temperature control was possible. Talk at the time that the paint scheme would last for over twenty years was proven wrong not by its quality but by changing requirements in which almost all RAF Hercules were to return for grey-green finish which in 1984 began to be again changed to a

XV210 *displays its initial two-tone brown and black coat.*

wrap-round style. Radio fits, station lights, wing spar and fuel tank modification and much more has been undertaken on the aircraft. The new, large hangar enabled work to be undertaken on VC-10s, Britannias and both RAF and civil Short Belfasts. By mid-1968 Marshall had undertaken work for 38 countries.

Since the late 1950s Viscounts in considerable numbers have been attended to, and they are likely to remain a summer sight working the Cambridge-Channel Islands service. Charter operators, executive aircraft and private fliers call on most days, and a liaison service between Pye Radio and Phillips at Eindhoven is run by Dassault Falcons or Beech King Airs. Helicopters — civil and military — whirr in from time to time. When the Battle of Britain film was made Spitfires, '109s' and the Mitchell staged through on their way to the south of France, Since May 1972 Cambridge has had a longer runway to make the opera-

tion of large aircraft safer. The old Teversham Lane has become part of the airfield. The 1980s have brought expansion including a very large new hangar built primarily for the company's work on executive jets. These have included Boeing 727s, One-Elevens and Boeing 707s. A trade long pursued has been the transporting of horses to many distant places, particularly during Tattersalls' autumn sales. The Aer Turas CL-44 then calls, sometimes a Skyvan, Argosy or a Vanguard.

Technical support to the RAF's Hercules fleet has been a major task for Marshall Engineering over twenty years, and November 1985 saw completion and delivery of the twenty-ninth and final stretched Hercules 3 produced by Marshall by the insertion of two sections to lengthen the C-130 fuselage. In 1985 the company won a further three-year contract to maintain the RAF fleet. Lockheed C-130 Hercules transports have also

**Above** *First horse transporter to call, silver and black Bristol Freighter 21 F-BCJM of SCAL on 1 May 1949.*

**Below** *Later equivalent, Britannia EI-BBH, slips in over Coldham's Lane.*

been overhauled for the Royal Swedish Air Force, Nigeria, Jordan, Saudi Arabia and Gabon among others. But it is the company's contribution to the Falklands' campaign for which it can always justly feel most proud.

On 16 April 1982, two weeks after the Argentinian invasion of the islands, Marshall was asked to design and deliver as rapidly as possible a Hercules variant able to be refuelled in flight. That would make possible supply of special items and personnel, at sea initially and in an 'air-bridge' role when the islands were retaken. By supreme effort and 24-hour working days the first aircraft with probe and feed lines above the fuselage, *XV200*, flew after a mere two weeks and returned to the RAF on 5 May. Promptly it was used for special deliveries to the Task Force at sea, and by means of a trailed hook snatched items from the sea.

Such was the speed and skill with which the Marshall team devised the air-air refuelling (AAR) Hercules C 1P that on 30 April, with an insufficient Victor tanker

XV195 *probed for South Atlantic service.*

force to meet surge of demands placed upon it, Marshall was asked to produce a tanker Hercules for in-flight refuelling into which over the next few weeks six Her-cules were hastily converted. Refuelling a Hercules from a Victor had proven difficult because of speed differentials. With the all-Hercules combination as well as Victor help a passenger and cargo run was established between Ascension and Port Stanley. That flight took twelve hours and was neither easy nor comfortable, but it was instrumental to the taking and holding of the Falklands, and remains an available, feasible proposition although the construction of the large airfield has opened the way for more conventional links with Port Stanley — and again Marshall has a large involvement.

Overseas reinforcement either of men or machines has long been a prime RAF task. Decline in the size of the 'Empire' has left sensitive outposts, and the Commonwealth could well request assist-ance. Rapid response capability is essential as was clear in 1982 and probably involves AAR and certainly

means lifting large quantities of men and equipment. Following the Falklands' conflict the Chiefs of Staff re-appraised movement needs, opting for a fleet of very large tanker-cum-transport aircraft. The USAF displayed the KC-10 Extender, military equivalent of the DC-10. Unit cost of those being high, the British opted for six Rolls-Royce-engined Lockheed TriStar 500s and later purchased another three from Pan American Airways.

Marshall, with Lockheed links, was the obvious choice to undertake the large development programme. Obtaining the contract meant a tough battle, then as soon as it was won erection commenced at Cambridge of a gigantic hangar, the metal frame being built by Boulton & Paul of Norwich who had previously worked on Marshall hangars. The resultant structure, the South works, is one of Europe's largest buildings and arguably the largest

without central pier supports.

On 16 February 1983 the first TriStar quietly touched down on the 06/24 6,446-ft runway, by which time conversion planning was underway. To convert the TriStars has been a tedious task for they differ from each other and were never planned with a tanker role in mind. But of one thing all can be sure, abundant evidence of high quality workmanship, ever a Marshall hallmark.

. The first converted TriStar, *ZD950*, which entered the hangar on 10 August 1983, first flew on 9 July 1985. Later that year it commenced service trials including flights at high all-up weights. At around 540,000 lb loaded, the TriStars' airfield requirements are such that few British airfields could accept them, and from Cambridge the aircraft fly lightly loaded. The second example, *ZD953*, made its first flight on 23 December 1985 and was handed over to the RAF on 24

*By arguably Europe's largest hangar of its type rests the third TriStar K1,* ZD951.

March 1986. It served with 216 Squadron (which re-formed on 1 November 1983) for evaluation. Between June 1983 and 1985 standard TriStars flown first by British Airways crews and from October 1983 partly by RAF personnel have, in unmodified form, been used on the Falklands' route which has meant a few TriStar repositioning flights involving Cambridge. So powerful are the TriStar engines that traffic lights have been erected on the roads passing the airfield to prevent incidents involving, in particular, high-sided vehicles.

Two versions of the RAF TriStar are envisaged, the K 1 tanker as represented by the first four examples, and two KC 1 tanker-cargo aircraft. Early examples will return to Cambridge for fitment of underwing in-fight refuelling pods for three-point AAR as well as for conversion to freighters.

Of all the aircraft that have passed through Marshall hands these majestic mammoths seem, by general consent, to be rated among the most beautiful and certainly are the most spectacular. Their power, their enormous strategic potential and delight upon the eye — for the RAF paint scheme suits them well – all combine to generate an almost hitherto unknown thrill among all who see them fly. Anyone excited by aeroplanes, upon which sensation I feel fairly placed to comment having enjoyed it for over half a century, would surely agree!

On a fair summer Sunday the Chipmunks and sole Husky of 5 Air Experience Flight flying ATC cadets usually slot into the Cessna activity. You'll probably see a Viscount, for 15,000 passengers yearly fly on the Channel Islands' services. For two years the unusual high aspect ratio wing Short SD 330s were involved but the Viscount managed to retrieve its place and oust the strange

*Pilot and instructor of the Cambridge University Air Squadron discuss business alongside a post-war Tiger Moth* (RAF Museum P100168).

newcomer on 29 July 1983. Marathons and DC-4Ms earlier were used on these flights. Dakotas too, and they were no new sight for Marshall overhauled RAF Dakotas during the Berlin Airlift. From Coldham's Lane the huge TriStar area is impossible to overlook, and maybe a Gulfstream 3 will be around. But the sight which must most readily please will surely be of the Tiger Moths of the Cambridge Private Flying Group whose shelter is a genuine wartime-sited Blister hangar. Look for *G-AEOI*, that Tiger which saw service in France in 1940. A fascinating thought if you stop to view flying at what must surely be the county's most interesting airfield.

Cambridge remains in the private hands of Marshall (Engineering) Ltd, a magnificent tribute to enterprise and tremendous hard effort. The firm's contribution to British aviation, largely unrecorded, has been truly great. At the helm remains Sir Arthur Marshall who has done much to maintain the very highest standards in aviation throughout the world. Little wonder the world's rich and famous have their aircraft overhauled here. Little wonder, too, that the accolade has been awarded to a very great man.

# Castle Camps

*TL630425. 3 miles NW of Steeple Bumpstead, to W of Camps Green*

Windswept and bleak, Castle Camps sits atop the East Anglian Heights. A few ruined huts and fragments of perimeter track remain, otherwise prosperous farmland marks the spot where history really was made. Here, on 26 January 1942, the magnificent Mosquito fighter (in dual control form) joined its first RAF squadron. One might have expected some visual token in memory of this great event; instead, open fields. Indeed, it is difficult for anyone who did not know Castle Camps in the flourishing days to even find its precise location.

Work on Castle Camps began in September 1939 and in mid-June 1940 it became Debden's satellite, an attachment which did not cease until Great Sampford became available in 1942. On 27 June 1940 85 Squadron began to use the open field where tented accommodation was made available. Then 111 Squadron, pulled out of the front line on 18 August 1940, rested at Castle Camps at the height of the Battle of Britain. Apart from East Coast scrambles, 'Treble One' had what they needed before returning south.

No 73 Squadron then arrived from Church Fenton and made Debden its home but was instantly transferred to Castle Camps, then known as F.1. Action was almost immediate. Some four hours after arriving on 5 September they engaged a raid over the Thames Estuary. The targets for the Luftwaffe were oil tanks at Thameshaven. It cost 73 Squadron one pilot killed, another wounded, three Huricanes shot down and three damaged, in return for which an He 111 of KG 53 had been damaged.

The sixth of September was a superb day as 73 Squadron was hurled into fierce action again over the Thames Estuary and North Kent, and Pilot Officer Marchand drew first blood, a Bf 109 of JG 26. Next day the Luftwaffe launched its first heavy day raid on London and in the Billericay area 73 Squadron engaged BF 110s, claiming three. Back at Castle Camps the pilots had to sleep in tents at the dispersals, and feed in a marquee set up in the woods, alongside which a hangar was later sited. Then they awaited the invasion, expected on 8 September. On the 11th they went into action again with 17 Squadron, against He 111s over the Isle of Sheppey. All and every day 73 Squadron was ready for action and on 15 September it intercepted a mid-morning raid over Maidstone, claimed two Bf 109s and shot down another low over the Blackwater estuary. At 14:45 hours the squadron was off again, the only six Hurricanes serviceable coming face to face with 100 German

*Castle Camps on 31 August 1940 seen from a nosey Dornier* (Charles Strickland, via P.H.T. Green).

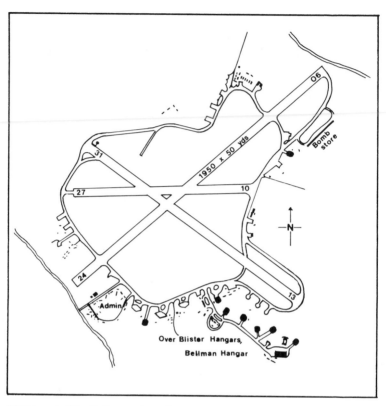

*1944 layout of Castle Camps. Imposing runways on to a satellite results in a strange layout. A solitary Bellman hangar is supplemented by eight Over Blister types. Domestic sites are scattered.*

bombers over Maidstone, three of which they claimed to damage.

The exposed siting of the satellite field meant that it was highly susceptible to strong winds which made flying tricky. On 21 September 73 Squadron began to be daily reinforced by 257 Squadron from Martlesham under Flight Lieutenant Stanford Tuck, which returned to its base at night. Two days later 17,73 and 257 Squadrons were 'bounced' over Kent and 73 Squadron lost five Hurricanes. A fierce encounter with Bf 110s came on

27 September and, into October, 17,73 and 257 Squadrons flew as a Wing. Then, on 23 October, 73 Squadron received the news that it was to become a night fighter squadron and Castle Camps became vacant in early November.

During 1941 the airfield was extended, better accommodation provided and runways laid. Although SHQ opened in 1941 it was 1942 before the black Mosquitoes came. Amid great secrecy the squadron worked up, surrounded by many amazing stories about the secret wonderplane.

One tale was that a notice in the cockpit reminded the pilot not to exceed 600 mph! The Mosquito for all its excellence was not a forgiving aeroplane and there were some unfortunate accidents. Worrying moments came when cowling panels were burnt through due to hot exhausts, but under Gordon Slade, later to become famous as a Fairey test-pilot, the bugs were worked out at an airfield loathed by its occupants. Why this wet place, which played havoc with the aircrafts' electrics, was ever chosen as the first Mosquito station remains a myster. Its proximity to de Havilland at Hatfield was one possible reason, another its relative remoteness in those days.

On 27 April 1942 crews of 157 Squadron were ordered on their first operational patrols, when a 'Baedeker raid' broke on Norwich. A few sightings were recorded, but little else resulted until 30 May when Squadron Leader Ashfield chased a Dornier 217, fired at it off Dover and claimed the first enemy aircraft to fall to 157 Squadron — but not to the Mosquito, for this prize went to 151 Squadron at Wittering. Confirmation of all these early claims is unlikely to be established now. Certainly four Do 217s were lost on 30 May. South coast radar lost trace of Ashfield's quarry, but a Do 217 came down off Holland and seems likely to have been his. No 157 Squadron was very unlucky for so many of their patrols and scrambles were fruitless. Not until 22 August did they have a proven success, a Do 217 which came down at Worlington.

On 15 March 1943 No 157 Squadron moved to Bradwell Bay, its place being taken by No 605 (County of Warwick) Mosquito squadron. It had only just received Mosquitoes, and used them mainly in the intruder role in which they were adding to 23 Squadron's Mosquito knowledge. In July 1943 (when Castle Camps became a satellite of North Weald) they began to use Mk VI fighter-bombers for intruder operations, doing so very effectively and scoring a number of successes. They flew *Rangers* widely over Europe, but their greatest contribution was the introduction of the Mosquito to bomber support duties. Their first such operation came on 31 August when they supported a Berlin raid. Four nights later they began *Mahmouds*, operations on the flank of the bomber stream designed to intercept enemy night fighters. The squadron left Castle Camps in October 1943, after having had some support from Mosquitoes detached from 456 Squadron.

Replacement for the dashing Mosquitoes was of an unexpected type, for it came in the form of Blenheim IVs, Hurricanes and Hornet Moths of 527 Radar Calibration Squadron here until February 1944, and dispersed in the north-east corner of the airfield. A few Blenheims wore the predominantly white scheme of Coastal Command, for operations over the sea.

February 1944 brought the unmistakable roar of Griffon Spitfires of 91 Squadron. They arrived flying Mk XIIs but whilst at Castle Camps received the Mk XIV, the second squadron to equip, and left on 17 March. Their immediate replacement was 486 Squadron flying Typhoons — but not for long. Early in April they began to re-arm with Tempest Vs and as part of 149 Airfield left on 29 April.

Whilst these two squadrons were re-equipping, Castle Camps had since the end of December 1943, housed Mosquito Mk XIIIs of 410 Squadron. This was a night home defence squadron guarding the northern approaches to London. When, on 21 January 1944, the enemy opened the 'Baby Blitz', No 410 Squadron was at once drawn into the night battle, having notable successes. This Canadian squadron stayed here to the end of April 1944.

There was a quiet spell before, in July 1944, 68 Squadron brought their Mosquitoes along, and stayed until October, during which time they made night interceptions of V-1s. A five-week stay beginning on 8 October was made by other

*Mosquito NF 30s of 85 Squadron at Castle Camps, April 1945,* VY:B-NT484 *nearest* (Charles Strickland, via P.H.T. Green).

Mosquitoes of 151 Squadron, and on 27 October 25 Squadron, also Mosquito-equipped, came for a sojourn which lasted until the station closed. Bomber support was their main activity and they were joined in this by 307 Squadron between the end of January 1945 and June. At the end of that month 85 Squadron came with Mosquito night fighters. On 28 July six of them escorted the Prime Minister's aircraft to the Potsdam Conference. They moved to Tangmere in October 1945.

The rear party of Station HQ left Castle Camps for Boxted on 17 January 1946, and the station, never again used for flying, closed in the summer. It was always a strange place. The main entrance was from the road leading beyond the village church, from which the airfield site can be viewed.

## Caxton Gibbet

*TL300605. At junction of A14(T) and A45(T) E of St Neots*
Night flying by Tiger Moths of No 22 EFTS took place at Caxton Gibbet before any such was undertaken, during the war, at Cambridge. In the early hours of 16 July 1941 Tiger Moths R4962 and R4968 were floating around the circuit when an intruder opened fire. Some flashes, and the trainers burst into flames, falling to the ground. The Germans came for a repeat performance on 6 August, and in style. After calling up the control van — there was never any control tower — made two approaches, circled and then on the fourth run deposited a stick of ten bombs across the landing ground damaging five 'Tigers' as a parting gesture.

It was in the summer of 1940 that the Air Ministry requisitioned a large grass

62

field, on the western apex of which still stands the inn by the hangman's gibbet at the junction of Ermine Street and the A45. The field was used from September as a Relief Landing Ground for 'circuit and bumping' Tiger Moths of 22 EFTS, thus relieving pressure on busy Cambridge. Then, in June 1941, 'F' Flight of the EFTS moved to Caxton, operating from there until well into 1944. It was a small field, but somehow a Wellington of 101 Squadron landed there on one occasion.

Huts along the northern edge of the landing ground were in 1944 taken over to accommodate personnel of 105 Squadron then at Bourn. Evidently the squadron had a skilled artist who decorated the hut walls with murals which could be seen into the 1950s.

# Duxford

*TL460460. 7 miles NE of Royston, Hertfordshire, by A505*

One sound, one sight supreme will forever be synonymous with Duxford. Of course, the Spitfire. Saturday, 30 July 1938 was a fine summer's day. As customary then Duxford closed at noon for the weekend. Sad, in a way, because something which would change the course of history was to take place.

Around 16:00, with few there to witness it, a Spitfire — the first for the RAF — whistled in as only a Spitfire could. A few fast aerobatics then *K9792* landed. The pilot was entertained to tea in the Mess, one may assume in that gracious style of pre-war days. Before leaving he flew the Spitfire again, presenting a stunning display to the watching few. Then the precious aeroplane was pushed into a hangar and 19 Squadron soon had its first Spitfire.

As the country passed through the sobering ordeal of the Munich crisis, 19 Squadron explored its new mounts and in November 66 Squadron also began to equip. No 19 had become the RAF's premier fighter squadron and Duxford's place in history was assured.

Visit Duxford and hangars of World War 1 style immediately greet the eye — if one can possibly overlook the giant 1985 construction which sits so incongruously, presumably trying to hide in a distant corner. Although the site which Duxford occupies is that of a First World War airfield used among others by RE 8s and DH 4s, almost all the buildings date from around the end of that war. Nearby at that time was an ever larger aerodrome at Fowlmere which in appearance resembled Duxford, except that its domestic site was adjacent to the technical site whereas a main road separates these features at Duxford. The other prominent Duxford hangar is a 'T 2' which was brought here from Tempsford and stands on the site of a former similar one erected, along with offices and buildings for technical uses, in the 1950s.

Duxford opened in 1919 and in June 1920 became the home of the 15 aircraft of No 2 Flying Training School which flew Avro 504s, F2Bs, and DH 9As before moving to Digby in July 1924. In 1923 a major review of the air defence of the United Kingdom had resulted in a dramatic change of role for Duxford, which became a fighter station charged with the defence of East Anglia and the East Midlands. To achieve this two squadrons, Nos 19 and 29, re-formed on 1 April 1923 equipped with Sopwith Snipes. At the end of the year they began to receive Gloster Grebes and in March-April 1928 Siskin IIIs. They had been joined by 111 Squadron which re-formed here on 1 October 1923 with Grebes and which, from June 1924, flew Siskin IIIs. 'Treble-One' became the High Altitude Squadron in 1926 responsible for developing equipment for high altitude fighting. It received Siskin IIIAs in September 1926 and in 1927 command of the squadron fell to Squadron Leader Keith R. Park, later of Battle of Britain and Malta defence fame.

On 1 April 1928 Nos 29 and 111 Squadrons vacated the station just after 19 Squadron received Siskin IIIAs. In September 1931, 19 Squadron re-

**Above** *Duxford, almost completed, viewed from the west* (RAF Museum P3755).

**Below** *Ah, the wonders of Duxford 1934 Empire Air Day, and a 99 Squadron Heyford to clamber into. Gauntlet K4089 of 19 Squadron was clearly over-awed, like me!* (Cambridgeshire Collection).

**Above** *Cambridge-based Tiger Moth G-AOEI with HIZ behind visiting Audley End, July 1977.*

**Below** *Hercules C3 XV219 in the Cambridge snow.*

**Above** *Hercules tended by Marshall swing into line over Wiltshire as they head for the 1977 Queen's Jubilee Review of the Royal Air Force.*

**Below** *RE8s were seen in some numbers over the county in the 1914-1918 war. A grounded example may be seen at Duxford.*

**Above** *Beautifully restored, a P-51 Mustang painted to represent one of the 78th Fighter Wing, Duxford. July 1974.*

**Below** *Great excitement surrounded the arrival and repainting of this ex-Indian B-24 pictured at Duxford in January 1975.*

**Above** *'Messerschmitt 109s' airborne from Duxford in 1968 during filming of* The Battle of Britain.

**Below** *Duxford's Meteor represents F8 WK991 of 56 Squadron based at Waterbeach.*

On parade, 19 Squadron's Gauntlets. The A10 heading easterly can be distantly glipsed (RAF Museum 5510-6).

equipped with Bulldogs. Since 1926 fighters here had been adorned with squadron colours, 19 adopting light blue in their markings because of its local associations.

In January 1935 19 Squadron became the first to equip with Gloster Gauntlets and, when 66 Squadron re-formed on 20 July 1936, it was similarly equipped. During the Munich crisis, Duxford's Gauntlets were armed and refuelled for conflict seeming imminent. Once the alarm had passed, both squadrons reverted to air drill, exploring the possibilities of the Spitfire, trying some night flying and detaching themselves to Sutton Bridge for armament training.

Duxford had long housed another unit, the Cambridge University Air Squadron formed on 1 October 1925 to interest undergraduates in the RAF. Its head-quarters — currently in Chaucer Road, Cambridge — were then in the Engineer-

ing Laboratories on Fen Causeway. At Duxford the squadron commenced practice flying in Avro 504s on 19 February 1926. It received a boost in 1933 when Avro Tutors – whose yellow forms graced Duxford to the outbreak of war – replaced the Atlas trainers.

Duxford was also the home of the Meteorological Flight which used Bull-dogs and in September 1936 re-equipped with four Gloster Gauntlets, before moving to Mildenhall on 2 November 1936.

Three Spitfire squadrons were at Dux-ford when the war commenced, the third being No 611 (West Lancashire) Auxil-iary Air Force Squadron here for its summer camp. All awaited a fight which did not occur, and on 10 October 1939 '611' impressively left for Digby, its Spit-fires breaking the intense security of those days by formating in such a manner as to describe '611' to those

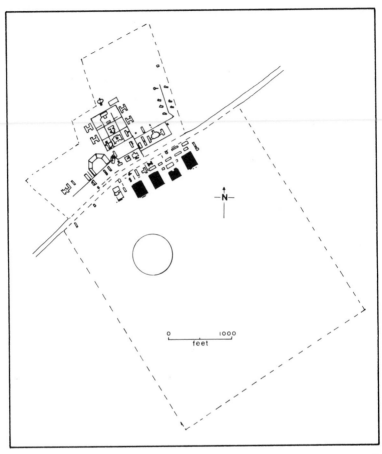

*Duxford's layout in April 1939. Four hangars (three double) are backed by a small technical site. Buildings across the main road form the domestic site.*

below! The squadrons left behind daily placed detachments at their forward airfield, Watton. On 20 October huge Ensign airliners impressed into service lifted the personnel of 19 Squadron for a short, rather unprofitable stay, at Catterick in the hope that it could interfere with enemy activity off the Yorkshire coast. No 66 Squadron, declared a mobile squadron on 25 October, expected to move to Leconfield. At the last moment the move was cancelled and in November both squadrons began placing detached Flights at the unfinished airfield at Horsham St Faith, near Norwich. On 11 January 1940 three Spitfires of 66 Squadron operating from Horsham engaged a Heinkel He 111 attacking shipping off Cromer, the bomber eventually crashing in Denmark. It was to Hor-

*'Cor, its an ENSIGN!' I only glimpsed one in wartime, in cloud, but they several times assisted moves of Cambridgeshire squadrons.* G-ADTC *in June 1940.*

sham St Faith, which both Duxford Spitfire squadrons continued to use as a forward airfield, that 66 Squadron eventually moved on 16 May 1940.

Placing Flights forward had allowed space at Duxford for the formation on 5 October 1939 of a new squadron, No 222, which in November began equipping with Blenheim IF long-range fighters. To this squadron, housed in the western hangar, came early in 1940 the famed legless pilot, Squadron Leader D. R. S. Bader, who became very much a Duxford figure.

In March 1940 222 Squadron received Spitfires. The suddenness of the May 1940 Blitzkrieg caught the squadrons unready. Defiants of 264 Squadron were quickly rushed to Duxford from Wittering and moved forward daily to operate from Horsham St Faith, the forward airfield for Duxford, whence they fought their first battles. Duxford's Spitfires operating from Horsham were involved in some tough action off Holland and, on 25 May, 19 Squadron went forward to Hornchurch to help cover the Dunkirk withdrawal during which the units fought hard before returning to Duxford on 5, June.

The satellite at Fowlmere came into use, 19 Squadron dispersing there. In June 1940 264 Squadron re-established itself after its hammering and moved to Fowlmere. Come July and 19 Squadron found that it had been chosen to try the cannon-armed Spitfire Ib. From the start these aircraft were troublesome, the main problem being cartridge ejection after the guns had fired. The squadron was told to persevere.

When the Battle of Britain opened 19 Squadron's cannon Spitfires were far from ready for action. Fortunately Duxford lay largely beyond the range of the daylight onslaught, nevertheless many patrols and scrambles took place and 19 Squadron fought off the East Coast. On 11 July Czech pilots arrived to form 310 Squadron, the first Czech fighter squadron for which Hurricanes began to arrive on 18 July. Its operations commenced on 18 August and the newcomers first engaged in battle on the 26th. It was 31 August, though, that was the most memorable day of this period.

On that glorious summer morning air raid sirens wailed over much of Essex and the area around Duxford. Could the

Luftwaffe be coming at last? I, for one, was soon without doubt as distant gunfire over Debden was joined by heavy firing from Duxford and Thriplow batteries. This sent the large work force heading on their cycles for Pye Radio, near my home, racing into air raid shelters. As I joined them there were tremendous explosions and, ten miles away from the source, the ground shook. Clearly, poor old Duxford was in trouble — or was it?

No, for part of a force of Dornier 17Zs was attacking Debden while the remainder headed for Duxford. The ferocity of the station's gunfire drove the raiders away and roughly between Fowlmere and Barrington, and with a few erratic overspills, they jettisoned their loads. Then they turned in a wide arc skirting the south of Cambridge and as they did so were engaged by 19 Squadron. Those wretched cannon, they cost the squadron dear for it lost two Spitfires in the face of fire from the Dorniers and escorting Bf 110s.

Much of the Battle of Britain fighting in which Duxford was involved took place in September 1940 when Leigh Mallory's 'Big Wing' ideas were tried. Squadrons from other 12 Group stations arrived each day, so that a Wing scramble was an amazing sight as literally scores of fighters raced away. Often Douglas Bader would be leading 242 Squadron. Hurricanes far outnumbered Spitfires during all operations from Duxford, from this period until late 1941.

No 310 (Czech) Hurricane Squadron was much in the fight during September. Its pilots waded into Do 17Zs and Bf 110s over North Weald on the 3rd and again on the 7th, making high claims. On the morning of the 15th No 310 was flying in the Wing with 19,242, 302 and 611 Squadrons in the defence of London and faced huge enemy formations. The two Spitfire squadrons went for the fighters leaving the bombers to the Hurricanes. 'A' Flight of 310 Squadron was unable to engage due to AA fire, but 242 and 'B' Flight of 310 Squadron waded in, engag-

ing the enemy at 22,000 ft over Kingston-upon-Thames. The afternoon brought another, more desperate fight since Bf 109s broke up the 'Big Wing' and so the squadrons fought on their own with 310 Squadron having to sort itself out after a climb to 24,000 ft. Then it faced a huge enemy conglomeration and claimed four raiders for the loss of two Hurricanes, one being that of Squadron Leader A. Hess, 'A' Flight Commander, who safely baled out. Duxford was at this time briefly hosting Poles of No 302 Squadron who claimed eleven bombers during the defence of London on that memorable day. By the end of the 15th Duxford's squadrons were claiming 44 enemy aircraft, eight more shared and eight probables, but the true total for the day was far less. Confusion had arisen during very complex engagements. It is unlikely that a totally accurate record of claims and losses will ever be compiled. Not until 27 September did 310 Squadron find itself in the thick of the fight again, and then distantly over Kent. Duxford's distance from the coast much reduced its value.

A second Czech squadron had formed at Duxford, No 312, but left in September. As the battle died down Duxford's value was assessed. It was too far from France for offensive operations and so 310 and 19 Squadrons were assigned to defensive patrols from the Duxford Sector.

On 1 December 1940 two Harrows, transports that before the war commonly crossed Cambridgeshire in their bomber days, touched down at Duxford bringing from Leconfield the ground crews of 258 Squadron. Their stay was but two days long for on the 3rd they were air-lifted in the opposite direction, to Drem in Scotland. A policy change was responsible, and the squadron went north to take over the Hurricanes of 263 Squadron.

December saw major change at Duxford. To free Northolt for offensive duties the Air Fighting Development Unit moved to Duxford joining 310. No 19 Squadron was soon based at Fowlmere. AFDU held some Spitfires and Hurricanes for tacti-

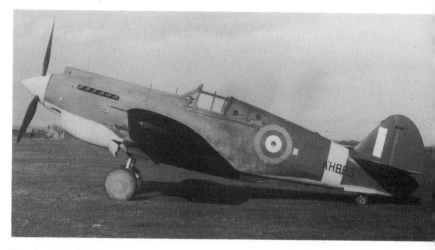

*Tomahawk 1* AH863 *early in 1941 at AFDU Duxford for evaluation* (via Bruce Robertson).

cal developments but its main task was to explore the fighting qualities of new types of aircraft, sometimes borrowed from squadrons. This brought the newly received American types, and the Naval Air Fighting Development Unit, alias 787 Squadron, which flew Fulmars, Martlets and Skuas from its dispersal area in the south-eastern corner and gave Duxford a cosmopolitan appearance. The procession of aircraft types made Duxford a spotter's paradise where one could gaze upon such rarities as the Maryland, Mohawk and the latest aircraft just entering service.

The Air Gun Mounting Establishment at Duxford between early 1941 and late 1942 also attracted interesting aircraft, including an Albacore, two Hawker Hectors (*K9714* and *K9772*), Gladiator *K8040*, Havoc *BJ474* in connection with upward firing guns German-style and, most exotic of all, the twin-finned Wellington 'II' *L4250* with a 40 mm gun in its huge dorsal turret. Its Duxford stay, 13 December 1941 to 24 January 1942,

occasioned much excitement.

On 26 June 1941 310's Hurricanes moved out and 56 Squadron's replaced them. The squadron flew a few offensive sorties, but it had come primarily to receive a new fighter, the Typhoon. In September 1941 it began to re-arm on a long torturous path to operations for the Typhoon was a troublesome aeroplane. Also to be seen was 601 (County of London) Squadron which arrived in mid-August 1941 when taking delivery of the Bell Airacobra, with which it fully equipped in October 1941. It was a strange aircraft for the engine was behind the pilot and the cannon fired through the propeller hub. Firing upset the compass so badly that the Airacobra had to be rejected and very few sorties, from Manston, were flown before the squadron left for Acaster Malbis in the first week of 1942.

On the southern side of the airfield Blenheim IVs, Hornet Moths and Cierva C30A autogiros of 74 Signals Wing were based, their task to calibrate coastal

**Above** *Airacobras of 601 Squadron at dispersal on the south side of Duxford.*

**Below** *ememnmy aircraft including Ju 88A-5 Werk Nr 6073 M2+MK of Kustenflier-gruppe 106 (later EE205) and captured at Chivenor formed a 'display circus' in autumn 1941* (via J. Robertson).

radar equipment. The autogiros arrived in summer 1940 and stayed until late 1942. Frequently they were away at radar stations.

Much excitement was aroused in September 1941 when a Heinkel He 111, a Ju 88, a Bf 109 and a Bf 110 arrived for tactical evaluation and demonstration to RAF squadrons. At the end of 1941 they were placed in No 1426 Enemy Aircraft Flight and dispersed in the airfield's south-west corner where ironically, decades later, part of *The Battle of Britain* film was made.

The main task in 1942 was to work the Typhoon into operational service. 56 Squadron was joined by 266 in January, followed by 609 in March, both of which equipped with Typhoons to create the Duxford Wing led by Wing Commander John Grandy. The Typhoons went into action in June and, flying from West Malling, were busy during the Dieppe landings. Gradually they moved to operational stations then, in the autumn, 181 Squadron formed at Duxford to try out the 'Bomphoon' before moving to the second satellite at Snailwell. The 'Hurri-bomber'

too had been first tried at Duxford where AFDU was still busy evaluating new types such as the Mitchell, Marauder and Ventura.

In October 1942 the 350th Fighter Group, USAAF, arrived at the station. Here briefly was the 345th Fighter Squadron. Others in the Group were sited at Coltishall and Snailwell. They brought an assortment of Bell Airacobras. Some ex-British and rejected were, technically, Bell P-400s. A few wore British camouflage but most had tan upper surfaces, a give-away to their likely destination. The motley collection was very active briefly before being flown, at the end of the year and via Gibraltar, for a part in Operation 'Torch', the landing in north-west Africa — hence their unusual colouring.

Activity at Duxford declined in 1943 although important trials of the Merlin Mustang *AM203* were underway, while the sight of that RAF Marauder provided magic moments for aeroplane watchers! During February and March AFDU moved to Wittering for the USAAF was about to completely invade what it came to call 'the Duckpond'. During the first

*Hurricanes of 56 Squadron at Duxford, summer 1941* (IWM).

*Mid-war brought the American 78th Fighter Wing and its Thunderbolts. Illustrated is P-47D WZ:0 of the 84th Fighter Squadron* (US Air Force).

week of April 1943 Republic P-47C Thunderbolts of the 78th Fighter Group noisily descended in strength. An unbelievable 75 aircraft was held by its three squadrons. The Americans endeared themselves much to the neighbourhood and worked up great affection for Duxford which many of them refered to as 'real antique'!

On 13 April 1943 the '78th' commenced operations, first claims being made on 14 May of two Fw 190s. P-47Ds came into use in June and long-range tanks were first operationally carried on 30 July, enabling the Thunderbolts to penetrate into Germany.

Strafing operations on a major scale commenced in January 1944, pilots returning with photo coverage of strikes on He 177s and Ju 188s hoping to operate against London at that time. The results were spectacular, and likewise

some of the first air-to-air combat film showing the Me 163 and Me 262 which the 78th engaged.

By D-Day an assortment of P-47Ds were in service, some with teardrop canopies. Cover to the Normandy landings was given and to the ill-fated Arnhem venture. A PSP runway was laid at Duxford in November-December 1944, during which time the 78th flew from Bassingbourn. Then it was 'all change' as the Group converted to flying P-51D Mustangs which it took into action for the first time on 29 December 1944.

April 1945 found the long-range Mustangs operating over Czechoslovakia, the final operation taking place on 25 April when the Group supported the RAF bombing raid on Hitler's famous lair at Berchtesgaden. In the course of 450 operations, 167 aircraft had been lost in action. Pilots of the 78th claimed 338 enemy aircraft destroyed in the air and 358 on the ground and shared one of each with other Groups.

Most of the Americans left Duxford in August 1945, the aircraft being disposed of around that time. Duxford then was held on care & maintenance until the end of the year when 165 Squadron began moving in with Spitfire LF 9s, the squadron's twelve aircraft arriving on 27 January 1946. In April 1946, 91 Squadron moved in with Spitfire 21s. No 165 Squadron staged a fly-past over the Channel Islands on 9 May, commemorating the liberation a year before, and both Spitfire squadrons participated in the Victory Fly-Past over London on 8 June. No 91 Squadron spent July and August 1946 at the Lübeck Armament Practice Camp and when it returned 165 Squadron was no more for, on 1 September 1946, it emerged as a new 66 Squadron and that, too, promptly visited Lübeck for training. On 20 November 1946 both squadrons began making use of Duxford's satellite, Debden whose hard runways were very useful as the squadrons converted late 1946 and into 1947 on to long nacelled, high-powered examples of the Meteor III.

The start of 1947 found 91 Squadron at APS Acklington and when it returned to Duxford and the front line on 15 February 1947 it did so as 92 Squadron for it had been re-numbered on 31 January 1947. No 66 Squadron became fully operational on Meteors in March. On 17 April No 56 Squadron, also flying Meteor IIIs, moved in from Wattisham. Until recently active as 124 Squadron, its aircraft still paraded the ON identity letters of that squadron. An interesting event was the arrival in September of Tempests of Nos 3 and 80 Squadrons, Wunstorf, and Meteors of 74 and 222 Squadrons all briefly here for a part in the Battle of Britain fly-past.

Major appraisal of fighter defence needs had been undertaking in January 1947. As a result, three short-range day fighter squadrons armed with 24 Meteor IIIs were now Duxford-based. By the end of the year, with the Meteor 4 in the offing, it was clear that Duxford could not readily accommodate that type because it lacked a permanent hard 2,000-yd runway. In order to operate Mk 4s, No 56 Squadron, on 1 February 1948, moved into the Thorney Island Wing. The following month found 92 Squadron, which early in the year had again been away at APS Acklington, once more detached, this time for armament training at Lübeck.

Both 66 and 92 Squadrons again vacated Duxford, in mid-May, and at a crucial time for they were in the throes of converting to Meteor 4s, the first of which reached both 66 Squadron and 92 Squadron on 6 May. While Duxford's metal runway was extended and repaired as a temporary measure the two squadrons worked up on Meteor 4s at Martlesham Heath from where they returned to Duxford on 10 June 1948.

Duxford was considered unsuitable for fast jets and plans now called for it to accommodate four Mosquito night fighter squadrons instead. The intention by now was that long-range intruders would be stationed at Coltishall and Wattisham, but re-appraisal of Duxford showed insufficient support facilities for Mosquito night fighters, so its role was switched with that of Coltishall.

Revised plans in 1949 called for two Hornet squadrons and later a Canberra intruder squadron to be sited at Duxford, after a 2,000-yd concrete 06/24 runway was laid. Meanwhile the Meteor squadrons trained in earnest, 66 and 92 spending February 1949 at Acklington and in June they participated in the large scale Exercise 'Foil' which highlighted alarmingly the inadequacy of Britain's air defences. Rapid take-off and Wing form-up were essential in order to engage the threat posed by vast Russian bomber formations, and therefore a decision was made to retain the PSP track runway at Duxford alongside any new runway. On 6 and 7 October 1949 both Meteor squadrons left Duxford for Linton-on-Ouse, after which the station was placed on care & maintenance. Funding for the runway was not availlable until the next year and on 18 September 1950 Messrs W. C. French began the task.

Terrorist activity in Malaya was such that all the Hornet intruders were ordered there, to serve as ground-attack aircraft. The intended jet intruder, the DH 110 Vixen, was years away and so the long-range intruder force disbanded. Its squadrons were given a day interceptor role and re-armed in 1951 with Meteor 8s. When in mid-August 1951 the 'intruder' squadrons moved in to Duxford, Nos 64 and 65 did so as day fighter squadrons.

At no time in its existence has the home fighter defence force been so appallingly neglected as it was in the late 1940s and early 1950s. The implications of the USSR's ever-increasing military potential were not responded to with conviction until the Korean War forced the government out of incredible complacency. By that time an armada of over 700 TU-4s, the Russian copy of the American B-29, had been produced; no mean achievement. Intelligence sources ascertained that its intention was, as suspected, to deal a shattering, sudden attack upon Britain and western Europe. So dangerous had the situation become long before Meteors returned to incomplete Duxford in 1951 that Exercise 'Fabulous' was well under way. All squadrons on a rota basis took turns standing by fully armed, carrying live ammunition and at instant readiness to intercept, if necessary even destroy, any unidentified aircraft venturing into British air space. Never before in peacetime had such a measure been implemented. By September 1951 the Duxford squadrons were participating in the quick reaction alert scheme which in varied styles still faces the continuing threat posed by the Soviet Union. With plenty of B-29s and B-50s in USAF hands to practice upon, many exercises were undertaken to develop and practice techniques needed to destroy their Russian equivalents. Included was the concept of Wing operation, Exercise 'Hopscotch', in which airborne Wings assembled after fast take-offs for which the PSP runway could be used by fighters scrambling simultaneously from two runways. During one such trial the 32 Meteors of the Duxford Wing were away in a mere 75 seconds.

*A 'real' Hunter, not a museum example. XF451 of 65 Squadron at Duxford.*

Duxford periodically housed detachments of Vampires from 2 TAF, usefully simulating jet bombers in practices. For the huge Coronation flypast over Odiham in July 1953 the station was temporary home for thirty RAF F-86 Sabres of Nos 3 and 67 Squadrons which joined the Meteor 8s of 64 and 65 in a massive

*Meteor 8s of 65 Squadron about to demonstrate rapid take off.*

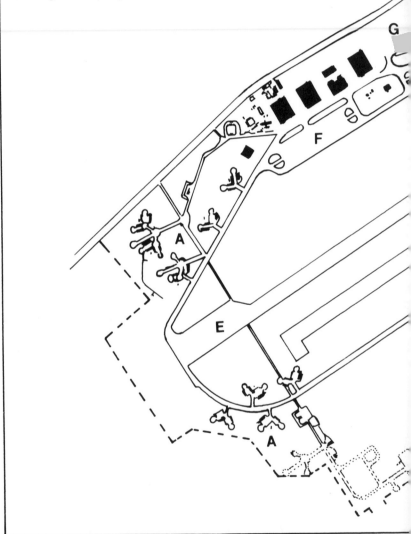

*Extended for the nuclear age, Duxford of August 1953. Areas A and B each support a squadron, blast walls flanking hardstandings. Projected dispersals for a third squadron (C) are shown dotted. D is the second PSP runway, E is the main runway with Operational Readiness Platforms (ORPs) at either end, F is the Aircraft Servicing Platform (ASP) and G an additional metal hangar.*

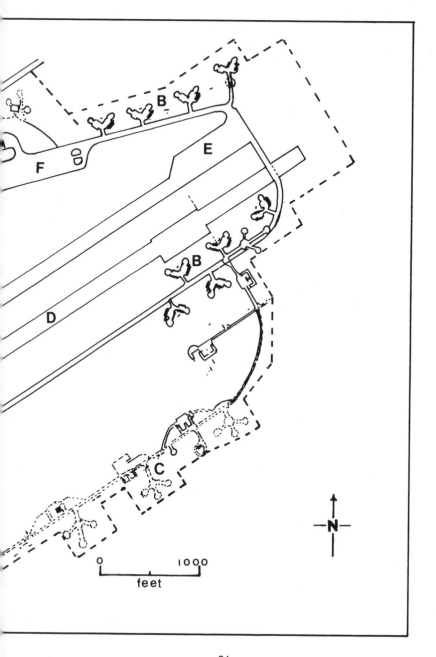

aerial parade, much of which assembled around Duxford as it headed for the Initial Point near Watford. Reminiscent it certainly was of that 1935 Jubilee event. Sadly, never again will so many RAF aircraft perform simultaneously.

The intention now was to re-arm 64 and 65 Squadrons with Hunters, then exchange both squadrons with Horsham St Faith's two squadrons of Swift 7s (Nos 74 and 245) armed with Fairey Fireflash beam-riding missiles for daylight operations against the TU-4s. The move was dictated by the Hunter's inferior range to that of the Swift. But the Swift proved a distressing failure and after the Duxford squadrons re-armed they stayed put. Instead, 64 Squadron was switched to a night fighter role and began equipping with Meteor NF 12s in August 1956 and by the end of the year was also using NF 14s. No 65 Squadron received Hunter 6s in January and February 1957, and flew its last operational Meteor F 8 sortie on 21 March 1957. Javelin 7s replaced 64's Meteors during September and October 1958, and all could be dispersed on

hardstandings — protected by blast walls — positioned at the four corners of the airfield. At each end of the runway readiness platforms and telescramble lines were in place for QRA purposes.

Javelin 9s with limited re-heat began replacing 64's Mk 7s in July and August 1960. No 65 Squadron disbanded on 31 March 1961. No further runway extension and necessary update was deemed feasible for the general state of Duxford's aged buildings left much to be desired. No 64 Squadron moved to Waterbeach on 28 July 1961.

On 31 July Air Vice-Marshal R. N. Bateson, leader of 613 Mosquito Squadron's famous 1944 low-level raid on Gestapo registry in the Hague, took off from Duxford in a Meteor T 7. To the distinguished officer had come the privilege of ceremoniously ending Duxford's active days as an RAF station. Some of the quarters were to remain in MoD use for some time, however.

It was generally assumed that flying from Duxford had ceased. Not so, for in 1968 the aerodrome suddenly and

*Duxford Javelin FAW 9, XH872 of 64 Squadron, in August 1960.*

astonishingly resounded again to a multitude of Merlins when it became the main centre for the making of *The Battle of Britain* film. Once more Spitfires chuckled their way home, along with a few Hurricanes. Strange mock-ups of both taxied about and most incongruously a fleet of 'Me 109s' and 'He 111s' dominated the ASP. Reliance upon Rolls-Royce engines was nevertheless almost total. During the ensuing summer the sight of a formation of sixteen 'Me 109s', and the so-called Heinkels sounding like Lancasters, awoke mammoth desire that such scenes must never end, as enthusiasts from far flocked to view the wonder. 'Old Duxford must never die', was the cry!

A group of young enthusiasts banded themselves together and formed the East Anglian Aviation Society. Largely thanks to their efforts the Imperial War Museum came to Duxford, as more and more aircraft settled at the aerodrome. Mr Haydon Baillie based his two Canadair T-33A jet trainers here and a Sea Fury, *CF-CHB*, adding spice to the proceedings. Time-expired aeroplanes such as a Ju

52, a P-51 used by the USAF and RCAF, a Gannet and an ex-51 Squadron Comet rolled in and then came a real, live B-24 Liberator provoking enormous interest. It was eclipsed only by a somewhat battered, turretless B-17G-105-VE, *44-85784* alias *F-BGSR/N17TE* and *G-BEDF*, privately obtained by Euroworld from the French and which arrived from Beauvais via Biggin Hill on 15 March 1975 to become that exotic, splendid delight, 'Sally B'.

News that the Science Museum wanted to place the first British Concorde at Duxford was greeted with very mixed feelings, and at a time when relations between the enthusiasts and officials reached an all-time low. Many enthusiasts who had done much to save Duxford sadly departed, and the Museum replaced them with the Duxford Aviation Society in order to attract enthusiastic support. By then Cambridgeshire County Council, with a record of total disinterest in anything aeronautical, involved itself, as Duxford passed through tragic weeks. Caring hands luckily rescued Duxford,

*Duxford's 'Sally B' on its rounds in 1985.*

*Memorable moment, as Duxford's B-52 arrives over the M11 motorway.*

beckoning an ever increasing array of exciting aeroplanes with 1986 bringing, at long last, the return of a flying Republic P-47 to the aerodrome. One of the fascinating things is to arrive there as in years long gone being uncertain of what may be on view, old or new. That the M11 has been able to hack its way through the runway is regrettable, but many of the nicest aeroplanes have as much dislike of runways as they clearly have of officials! Duxford attracts visitors from all over the world and, despite the garden seats, is one of the few aerodromes where you can hide away between ancient buildings and hear wonderful sounds and glimpse wonderful things. You can also dream of great days, fabulous moments the station can recall, and perhaps detect a smell of dope and petrol while a Kestrel passes, even echoes in a proper hangar. You cannot afford to miss it.

## Fowlmere

*TL415440. By B1368*
Mere memory now, the airfield — or should it be airfields? — at Fowlmere.

The first opened as a training establishment in 1918, ending its days as a store place for hefty HP 0/400s in hangers like those still seen at Duxford but which were demolished in 1923. The second airfield was on a different site, and quickly developed in the spring of 1940. Possibly the Germans had rapid knowledge of it, for in mid-June 1940 they rained incendiaries on to a field at nearby Newton in the first bombing of Cambridgeshire.

Originally known as G.1 (each Fighter Sector Station had a letter identity and its satellite stations a number) it opened in June 1940. Spitfires of 19 Squadron, Duxford, began dispersing here on 1 July. Apart from tented accommodation nothing else marked the grass area as an airfield.

Three days later 19 Squadron returned to Duxford, making way for Defiants of 264 Squadron. Working back into operational state, it detached Sections for East Coast convoy patrols out of Martlesham, and investigated possible use of the Defiant for night fighting before leaving for Kirton-in-Lindsay on 23 July 1940. Two days later, 19 Squadron resumed

84

**Above** *The original Fowlmere, 6 June 1918* (Marshall Engineering).

**Below** *DH 9A* E9664 *at Fowlmere, August 1918* (Captain D.S. Glover, via P.H.T. Green).

*A Spitfire of 19 Squadron at Fowlmere* (RAF Museum P012502).

using Fowlmere, sending Sections to Coltishall for East Coast patrols.

During August, 19 Squadron was partly dispersed at Fowlmere where Spitfire Ibs stood ready for the action which came on 19 August, when Green Section claimed three Bf 110s. The squadron engaged Bf 109s on the 24th and on 31 August rose to protect Debden and Duxford during large-scale enemy activity in the area. Through September and October Spitfires of 19 Squadron flew as part of the 'Big Wing', usually staying away from the parent station during the day because so many aircraft daily assembled at Duxford. One cannot segregate '19' from Duxford. In those days it was synonymous with the station, whence it fully returned in November 1940. Hurricanes of 310 Squadron as well as 19's Spitfires dispersed at Fowlmere (now known as WA1), before 19 Squadron moved in on 6 February 1941 as AFDU needed more space at Duxford.

Standbys, interception patrols, sector patrols, reinforcement flights into 11 Group to replace fighters operating over France, these were daily routine for the squadron that defended Cambridgeshire.

In May 1941 it commenced sweeps across the Channel, taking part in a *Circus* for the first time on 21 May. Enemy reaction was spasmodic and not until 23 June did Fowlmere Spitfires tangle with Bf 109s, claiming two destroyed. Thereafter action became more intense, 19 Squadron being engaged in battle against Bf 109s near St Omer on June 27.

Offensive operations continued and on 12 August the squadron had an early call. It met, off Holland, Blenheims which had ventured to Cologne in daylight. A fierce battle ensued off Schouwen. On 16 August, 19 Squadron took off from Fowlmere for the last time, flying to a new home at Matlask.

No 19's place was taken by the third US Eagle squadron whose Hurricane IIbs arrived at Duxford in August and moved almost immediately to Fowlmere. The Americans saw little activity and spent a brief time at Wittering before moving to Eglinton, Northern Ireland, on 4 October.

A new squadron, No 154, formed at Fowlmere on 17 November 1941, flying Spitfire IIs. It flew forward base patrols from Coltishall and Swanton Morley, having made its first scramble from Fowlmere in February 1942, and moved to Church Stanton on 7 May. 174 Squadron was at Fowlmere in July, and 'Treble One' arrived with Spitfires on 27 September

*Conington aerodrome, February 1929. A field, shed and two visiting Bluebirds, G-AABE and G-AA0? (Cambridgeshire Collection).*

1942 and almost immediately went on leave. On return the squadron personnel were given tropical kit, said goodby to their Spitfires and left by train to their port of embarkation for North Africa.

Auster 1s of 655 Squadron were based here in February-March 1943 having arrived from Gatwick. Then came Fowlmere's part in Exercise 'Spartan', testing the mobility of the tactical element of Fighter command. This brought 411 Squadron's Spitfire Vs to Fowlmere for a brief stay in March 1943. Their place was taken on 19 March by 2 Squadron's Mustang Is from Bottisham. Ten days later they commenced *Lagoons* off Texel, operating quite intensively during April, in pairs, before returning to their native Sawbridgeworth on 27 April.

The task now was to extend the airfield and add two Sommerfeld track runways and a 'T2' hangar to the seven Blister hangars already here. Fowlmere then became Station 378 USAAF. April 1944 brought the Americans with P.51Bs, the 339th Fighter Group flying its first sweep on 30 April. Five weeks of fighter escorts were followed by mixed operations including heavy and medium bomber escorts, interdictor operations and ground strafing. It provided fighter cover

over Normandy's beaches and strafed during the St Lô break-out. The Group's P-51Ds gave cover during the airborne landings in Holland as well as flying offensive patrols during the Ardennes battle and also during the Rhine crossing. Final sorties were flown on 21 April 1945.

This Fighter Group, the 339th, claimed over 200 enemy aircraft shot down and 400 destroyed on the ground during 264 operations. After the war the green-nosed P-51s were still a common sight, but by August 1945 the unit was winding down fast and eventually left for America in October that year. Fowlmere withered away by the end of 1945 and was sold in 1957.

## Glatton

*TL185870. Off A1 11 miles N of Hunting-don, on B660 near Conington*

Conington village knew the sound of aeroplanes long before Glatton airfield was built, for the Suffolk and Eastern Counties Aero Club established a small outpost here where, in November 1928, the Cambridge Aero Club was initiated. On Mondays and Thursdays two Black-burn Bluebird II or III biplanes would arrive, often carrying a passenger for

**Above** *B-17G 'Mission Maid' of the 457th BG, at Glatton on 1 January 1945 after its 75th mission* (US Air Force).

**Below** *Combat Mess at Glatton, 17 March 1945* (US Air Force).

*The 457th celebrates the victory, around Glatton's tower, 11 May 1945 (US Air Force).*

50/- return between Ipswich and Conington. It was a brief venture, for Conington closed in March 1929. Marshall's Cambridge aerodrome replaced it.

Glatton, constructed by US Army engineers in 1943 and completed with two 'T2' hangars, was taken over by the USAAF late that year. The 457th Bomb Group arrived late in January 1944 and flew B-17Gs. Its first operation took place during the 'Big Week' on 21 February 1944. Thereafter the Group concentrated on strategic targets until June 1944 when they participated in softening up operations prior to the Normandy landings, and bombed defences in the Cherbourg Peninsula. During June 1944 they attacked airfields, roads and railways before switching to strategic targets in July. Such raids continued until the final operation, the 237th, on 20 April 1945. The Group then participated in Operation 'Exodus', the repatriation of PoWs from France and Austria, before leaving for the USA in June.

On 5 July the base passed from the 1st Air Division Substitution Unit (which occupied vacant US bases after the Group left) to 3 Group, RAF Bomber Command, to be prepared for the trooping of personnel to the Middle East, planning calling for up to 20,000 personnel to pass through the station each month. Late in August 1945 Liberators and Lancasters, mainly Upwood-based, began using the station, but not at the forecast rate for, by the end of December, only 1,149 personnel had been flown out and 174 in, No 70 Transit Camp accommodating them. Quite a number of Liberators were brought here from the Mediterranean Theatre before Glatton passed to care & maintenance on 30 April 1946 and closed soon after.

The airfield is now known as Peterborough Airport, part of a wartime runway being used for light aircraft. A memorial to the 457th can be seen in Conington churchyard.

# Gransden Lodge

*TL293555. SE of Little Gransden on B1946 W of A14*

Few Canadian squadrons flew from Cambridgeshire airfields. A long-stay exception was No 405 (Vancouver) Squadron which for two years operated from Gransden Lodge, an airfield which straddled county boundaries and was officially addressed as being in Bedfordshire. A typical wartime station well dispersed and set amidst fields, it had the customary three runways, '036' of 2,000 yd and two of 1,400 yd. There were two 'T2' hangars and a 'B1', and 36 hardstandings were built here. This was a smaller station than many with accom-

modation for 86 officers, nearly 200 NCOs and over 800 airmen. Quarters were also available for nearly 300 WAAFs.

It opened as satellite to Tempsford early in 1942, No 1418 Flight arriving on 8 April from the parent station as the first unit to use Gransden. The Wireless Investigation Flight, detached from 109 Squadron, arrived, becoming 1474 Flight on 4 July 1942. Both units flew Wellingtons, the former conducting trials of *Gee*, the navigation aid. No 1474 Flight became 192 Squadron on 4 January 1943 shortly after receiving Wellington Xs and a few Mosquito IVs.

No 1418 Flight conducted various trials with bombers and on 20 July 1942

*Gransden Lodge, 1944. Basically usual layout, two 'T2' hangars and a Type 'B1'. Note circular hardstandings.*

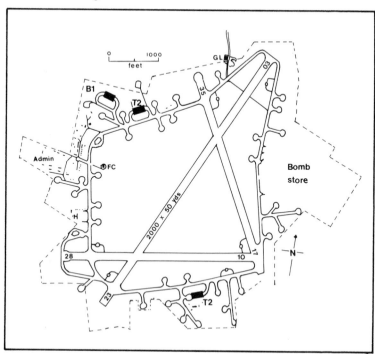

was absorbed by the Bombing Development Unit which then formed with four heavy bombers (two Stirlings and two Halifaxes), six Wellington IIIs and a Proctor. Trials of a technical nature were conducted by BDU, including a lot of work with H2S radar and radar for fighter defence in bombers. This unit and 192 Squadron moved to Feltwell early in April 1943, Gransden then switching from 3 to 8 Group and becoming the second satellite of Oakington on 15 April.

On 19 April the Pathfinder Navigational Training Unit formed at Gransden equipped with Halifax IIs and moved to Upwood and Warboys between 11 and 19 June 1943, the transfer being brought about because 405 Squadron had arrived with twenty Halifax IIs in April 1943, to join the Pathfinder Force. They flew their first operation from Gransden, against Duisburg, on 26 April. On 2 August 1943 the squadron began to operate Lancasters then, from the start of September, flew only Lancaster operations. The most famous Canadian-built Lancaster, *KB700* 'Ruhr Express', flew fifty sorties from Gransden.

Whilst runway work was undertaken at Bourn, 'B' Flight of 97 Squadron lodged at Gransden in August-September 1943, then left the station to the Canadians who intensively operated in the 'backer-up' role to the end of hostilities. No 1517 BAT Flight also used Gransden in 1943.

On 25 October 1944, 142 Squadron re-formed here with Mosquito XXVs as part of the LNSF, and operated with amazing efficiency. It flew 1,221 sorties

during 169 operations - 61 of them against Berlin — and lost only two aircraft. Another three were destroyed in crashes and two written off after battle damage.

As the war was ending the squadron became first to receive Mosquito B 35s, but disbanded on 28 September 1945. No 692 Squadron had arrived on 4 June 1945, replacing No 405 which left for Linton-on-Ouse on 26 May. No 692 Squadron disbanded on 20 September 1945.

December 1945 saw the arrival of transport Liberators of 53 Squadron. Its stay was short, most personnel leaving on 10 February 1946. The last Liberator returned from trooping on 20 February 1946, and the squadron disbanded on 1 March 1946. The station's main runway, 04/22 and 2,000 yards long, was maintained into the 1950s for emergency use and also because Gransden had been earmarked as a post-war bomber station.

# Graveley

*TL238645. W of Graveley village off A14*
*4 miles S of Huntingdon*

It remains incredible that such a small aeroplane as the Mosquito could carry a bomb as large as a 4,000-pounder, which represented a fifth of the all-up weight of the combination. But carry that load Mosquitoes did, and many times from Graveley whence this heavy load was first delivered to the foe.

De Havilland suggested modifying the Mosquito's bomb bay for the 4,000-pounder during April 1943. Seven weeks

*4,000 lb 'cookies' about to be loaded in Mosquitoes of 692 Squadron at Graveley (BAe).*

later a trial installation was ready for tests. Originally 627 Squadron was to pioneer the aircraft, but on 2 February 1944 the first two modified Mk IVs arrived at Graveley for 692 Squadron formed there on 1 January 1944 in the new Light Night Striking Force of 8 Group. On 23 February three Mosquitoes set off for Düsseldorf, each carrying one of the large bombs and thenceforth the Mosquito could crush as well as sting, and with exceptional accuracy. By night and day Mosquitoes operated, and often when the rest of Bomber Command was grounded. Graveley had FIDO which 8 Group made good use of when fog descended over the Group stations. By the end of hostilities No 692 Squadron had despatched 3,148 sorties and lost only sixteen Mosquitoes.

Graveley came into use as a satellite of Tempsford when 161 (Special Duties) Squadron arrived from Newmarket on 1 March 1942, 'A' Flight equipped with Lysanders and 'B' Flight with Whitley Vs. The later operated from here and Tempsford and the Lysanders from forward bases, until the squadron moved to Tempsford in April 1942. On 4 August 1942 Graveley came under the control of Wyton and the Pathfinder Force, 1504 BAT Flight bringing its Oxfords in for a week's stay before leaving for Honington on 14 August. Next day from Linton-On-Ouse and 4 Group came Halifax IIs of 35 Squadron which was based here for four years. Wyton relinquished Alconbury on 12 August and now had Graveley whose extensive activities, little publicly recorded, are worth examining.

The principal task for 35 Squadron was to mark and back-up with flares or large incendiaries the Pathfinder Force leaders, ten aircraft commencing such activity on 18/19 August against Flensburg. The three such raids, 26 sorties flown in August, cost the squadron three aircraft. On 5 October Squadron Leader J. C. Kerry, 'A' Flight Commander in *W1047:B*, failed to return, and a Halifax south of Cambridge suffered a spectacular lightn-

ing strike which temporarily blinded a crew member. The Cologne raid of 15 October, during which 250 lb 'Pink Pansy' incendiaries were dropped, cost four aircraft. Ten nights later the first raid to Italy (Milan) took place and on 6 November the squadron went minelaying, a rare event for '35'. Wing Commander B. V. Robinson, Squadron Commander, was on 18 November in one of eight aircraft operating against Turin. As he returned over the Alps a 'hung up' flare burst into flares so he ordered his crew to bale out. Soon the fire was out and so single-handed he flew *DT488:S* to Colerne.

Three raids were launched against Turin in December and on the 11th icing was so severe that only Sergeant R. E. Wilkes reached the target. His Halifax was seriously damaged by flak when on the 20th Duisburg was the target. Bombs were jettisoned, then a Ju 88 pestered the Halifax. An eventful journey indeed. No 35 Squadron mounted 29 raids from Graveley in 1942 despatching 237 Halifaxes and losing eight.

Berlin was first attacked from Graveley on 16/17 January 1943 but most raids then were against Lorient. By March 1943 the squadron was operating 'Z' aircraft (without nose turrets) and three times raided Berlin that month. When, on 20 April, Stettin was bombed Pilot Officer W. S. Sherk's aircraft was hit by incendiaries. He lost control and two crew members baled out — then he regained control. That month La Spezia was twice raided, in nine-hour flights, and on the 16/17th the long haul to Pilsen's Skoda works was undertaken, an operation repeated on 13/14 May by which time a number of Halifax Mak II srs ia with clear noses were in use.

Memorable at that time was the night of 4/5 May. Six aircraft had set off for Dortmund, their almost simultaneous return causing confusion in the circuit. Flight Sergeant J. A. Cobb in *DT489:Y* crashed on approach, all aboard dying except the rear gunner. Sergeant J. J.

Williams then ran out of fuel, and the crew baled out of *W7887:E* which crashed at Culverston. A more disastrous night was 29/30 May when four aircraft failed to return from Wuppertal. Even worse happened on 21/22 June when five of the nineteen which set out for Krefeld failed to return, and in addition Flight Lieutenant D. H. Milne was forced to ditch *BB368:H* off Cromer. Flak on the way in damaged the Halifax which was then attacked by a fighter. As it crossed the Dutch coast the bomber received further flak damage, and the crew were luckily snatched from the sea. In June Station HQ opened at Graveley, which had become completely divorced from Wyton.

Four times 35 Squadron attacked Hamburg in July's horrific onslaught. On 16 August 1943, 22 Halifaxes raided Turin and next night ten crews participated in the Peenemunde operation. Berlin was raided on 16 August, and of 23 aircraft sent three returned early and four were missing. On 31 August Squadron Leader Surtees failed to return from yet another Berlin raid, his aircraft *HR878:J* crashing in the Ijsselmeer. Some twenty years later he was taken to the spot, now polder and a wheat field where his aircraft had crashed. Much was found in the wreckage in good condition, among the items being the fire axe which Surtees had used to get out of the sinking bomber. Gerrit Zwanenburg's skill in locating and retrieving this and other items at the time proved to be a pathfinding act of another sort, largely leading to what has become known as 'aviation archaeology', although Gerrit's work is of an official nature.

An important night for '35' was 15/16 September. Montluçon was the target and for the first time the squadron provided the Master Bomber to control the raid, Wing Commander D. F. E. C. Dean flying *HX157:H*. Although the squadron continued to fly mainly Mk IIs it had a few Halifax IIIs, *HX232*, the first, arriving on 4 October.

When operations from Britain were flown against distant targets they were at the time regarded with awe by a population many of whom had barely strayed from their birthplace. Imagine then the thoughts of many when, on 11/12 November 1943, a nine-hour journey to Cannes on the 'French Riviera' was flown. Two aircraft were shot down whereas Pilot Officer J. R. P. Andrews had to ditch his aircraft ever further away from home — off Sardinia.

Twice in November and three times in December Berlin was raided. On 20 December 21 aircraft were despatched to Frankfurt. As Squadron Leader J. Sale, DSO, was circling prior to landing a target indicator still aboard exploded and burnt in the bomb bay. Sale ordered his crew out and five left the aircraft. The mid-upper gunner was unable to do so for his parachute had been burnt. With great skill and courage Sale managed to land the burning aircraft and taxi it off the runway. The two occupants were 200 yards away before *HX325:J* exploded.

January's poor weather reduced operations to seven, including a raid on Magdeburg on the 21st/22nd which cost three aircraft. A further three failed to return on 19/20 February when Leipzig was the target. By then the squadron knew that it was soon to have Lancaster IIIs. It flew its last Halifax raid, made by eighteen aircraft against Stuttgart, on 1/2 March 1944. On 6 March the first Lancaster, *ND643*, arrived from Wyton, Bourn's 97 Squadron contributed some and operations started on the 15th when twelve attacked Stuttgart. First away was Squadron Leader R. T. Fitzgerald in *ND597-TL:A*. Having Lancasters meant that 35 Squadron would drop large bombs and often 4,000-lb cookies. From Graveley the Halifaxes had mounted 159 attacks losing 63 aircraft in the course of 1,736 sorties showing a loss rate of 3.6% — lower than many squadrons.

The ninth of April 1944 saw the first raid from Graveley against a French pre-invasion rail target and by the month's ending Lille and Rouen had been bombed. When Laon was the target on the 22nd, Wing Commander S. P. Daniels was Master Bomber in *ND697:T* and Squadron Leader E. K. Creswell his Deputy in *ND755:B* Four nights later Graveley featured in a traumatic event. Lancaster *ND734* had just landed from Essen when a 692 Squadron Mosquito, its radio out of action, touched down then crashed into the Lancaster, killing a gunner.

Again, in May 1944, 35 Squadron provided the Master Bomber, for operations against railway installations in Lens, Trappes, Bourg Leopold and Montdidier and in the early hours of 6 June Lancasters attacked heavy guns at Maissy and Longues. Eleven times in June 1944 the 'master of ceremony' was provided by 35 Squadron, including a significant raid of the 25th when the squadron made its first Lancaster day raid with Motorgueil the target. Thereafter day raids were interspersed with night operations. Squadron Leaders Cresswell and Chigny acted as Master and Deputy Master Bombers for the Villenneuve raid of 4 July, and two days later Wing Commander P. H. Cribbins directed the Siracourt attack and Flight Lieutenant H. J. Hoover the bombing of Mimoyecques. Late the following evening Daniels and Cresswell controlled the massive assault on German land forces near Caen prior to an assault by land forces.

Throughout the summer 35 Squadron continued similar operations and then played a part in the reduction of Calais and Le Havre. By November day raids to Germany were frequent and then, on the evening of the 21st, 35 Squadron for the first time despatched two *Oboe*-equipped Lancasters for an attack on Wesel. Another unusual raid was that of the 4th when in daylight eighteen Lancasters attempted to destroy the Heinsbach River Dam.

Ever-present with large numbers of aircraft operating, sometimes through cloud, was the possibillity of collision and for 35 Squadron it came on 23 December 1944. Ten Lancasters set off for the Gremburg marshalling yards near Cologne and over the sea there was a tremendous explosion when *PB678:F* and *PB683:H* collided, killing all their occupants. Both the *Oboe* lead aircraft, *PB367:Z* and *PB372:X*, were seriously damaged by flak, also *PB685:J*. Undaunted,'35' set off for Cologne next day and this time *ME336:S* crashed shortly after take-off. By the end of 1944 the Lancasters had flown 1,657 sorties during 158 attacks which cost eighteen aircraft, the loss rate having been halved.

Many of the 1945 operations were directed against fuel installations. There were still deep penetrations, to Magdeburg, Chemnitz and Dresden in the attack upon which ten crews took part. The last bombing operation came on 25 April when guns on Wangerooge were raided by eight aircraft. Then came food drops to the Netherlanders. Lancasters flew 2,272 bombing sorties from Graveley, and in the course of 222 attacks, 24 aircraft were lost.

Meanwhile 692 Squadron had been intensively engaged in the fight, having visited Berlin no less than 111 times. Its final raid, on Kiel, took place on 2 May. Then it moved to Gransden on 4 June 1945, making room for more Lancasters and leaving 35 Squadron to contemplate a part in Tiger Force for the Far East while also pondering upon its peacetime role. In June 1945 No 227 Squadron's Lancasters moved in but disbanded on 5 September, making way for 115 Squadron.

Graveley had, perhaps surprisingly, been selected for development as a permanent station. Spring 1946 saw 35 Squadron equipping with black-and-white Lancaster B 1 (FE)s originally intended for Tiger Force and now replacing older aircraft. Summer was spent improving formation flying and in July-August it undertook a prestigious tour of the USA. The squadron's stay at Graveley after returning was brief, the station closing in September following a policy change. Both squadrons took their Lancasters to Stradishall.

For many years the station was held on care & maintenance. In the mid-1950s it returned to life as a Relief Landing Ground for 5 FTS, Oakington. The last aircraft to make use of it did so on 16 July 1964. Graveley closed to flying on 1 December 1968.

# Kimbolton

*TL 105695. 1 mile N of Kimbolton, on the Kimbolton to Spaldwick road*
Kimbolton was prepared in 1941 as Molesworth's satellite and on 29 November received Molesworth's first aircraft, a Wellington IV destined for 460 Squadron. Thereafter Kimbolton and Molesworth shared 460 Squadron's Wellingtons until early January 1942 when they left for Breighton.

Many Midlands airfields were being surveyed for American bombers. Inspection of Molesworth and Kimbolton during January 1942 resulted in agreement that both should be offered to the Americans for B-17s. An opening-up party arrived at improved RAF Kimbolton on 31 July 1942 and, on 13 September the 91st Bomb Group brought to Britain some of the first B-17Fs, their noses having increased clear transparency area and more pointed shape.

Placing Bassingbourn's Wellington's within the inland training area released their station, recently provided with hard runways, for offensive duty. These facilities were readily accepted by the comfort-conscious visitors who left Kimbolton for the splendour of Bassingbourn during October. Transit personnel on their way to 'Torch' replaced them. Statements that the 91st left Kimbolton because its runways could not withstand B-17 operations are only partly true. The

*Small ceremony, great event. The 379th Bomb Group takes over Kimbolton from the RAF, June 1943 (US Air Force).*

*Splendid line up! B–26 Marauders visiting Kimbolton on 24 November 1943 (US Air Force).*

main reason was to allow for expansion to accommodate a four-squadron USAAF bomber group.

On 30 March 1943 the station was again divorced from Molesworth and on 20 May 111 officers and 1,646 men of the four squadrons of the 379th Bombardment Group arrived. On 21 May another 115 officers and 203 enlisted men moved in. Six days later more came from AAF Station 109, Podington, then came B-17Fs on 21 May for the 379th BG. At noon.

*A contractor's party ponders the construction of a dispersal area at Kimbolton on 3 March 1944. It all looks a trifle primitive! (US Air Force).*

on 1 June 1943, Kimbolton was transferred to USAAF control, under Colonel M. Preston.

The 379th's operational deput came on 30 June during an attack on U-boat installations at St Nazaire. Operations by the Group included attacks upon strategic targets such as factories, oil plants, storage depots, submarine pens, airfields, communications centres and industrial items in distant Poland and Norway. Special raids were mounted against the IG Farben chemical plant in Ludwigshafen, an aircraft factory at Brunswick, the ball bearing works at Schweinfurt and synthetic oil plants at both Merseburg and Gelsenkirchen. The 379th played its part in the 1st Air Division's operations leading to the Normandy landings, the Arnhem assault, the Battle of the Bulge and the Rhine crossing and flew its final sorties on 25 April 25 1945.

The tally of operational sorties reached 10,492, bomb tonnage dropped 26,459 and number of operations, the record 330. Of the 379th's aircraft, none became better known than B-17G *42-40003-WA:H*, named *Ol' Gappy* and credited with 157 operational sorties. The 379th vacated Kimbolton on 16 June 1945.

After the Fortresses had gone, the runways and perimeter track echoed to the sound of marching by RAF new entrants posted to the recruit training centre here. The airfield hit the headlines in November 1971 when an abortive attempt was made by a Syrian flying a Piper Cherokee to smuggle immigrants into Britain.

# Little Staughton

*TL 120615. 4 miles W of St Neots, N of Bushmead*

Pforzheim was rarely attacked. A raid by 250 aircraft of 1 Group and fifty of 6 Group was thus an unusual event. Additionally, 8 Group, the Pathfinders, fielded another 53 aircraft as well as eight Lancasters of 582 Squadron, Little Staughton. One was flown by the Master

Bomber, Captain Edwin Swales, DFC, South African Air Force. Barely had his 'M-Mother' *PB538* reached the target area, when a fighter engaged the Lancaster. Although the rear guns were put out of action, Swales continued his task. A German fighter then repeatedly attacked and soon two engines were out of action.

Swales, his task completed, set course for home in an almost defenceless aircraft. By the time friendly territory was reached it became clear the aircraft could never land safely. Swales decided that his crew must bale out, which meant flying the aircraft steadily. Moments after the last man parachuted away *PB538* crashed at Chapelle au Bois, near Monchaux in France. Swales was killed and posthumously awarded the Victoria Cross.

On 1 December 1942, 475 American airmen and 28 officers arrived at Little Staughton to prepare the Advanced Air Depot, 1st Bombardment Wing, which positioned B-17s at this airfield, AAF Station 127. Little Staughton had previously attracted a variety of aircraft, the first to land being an Anson from Finningley which called on 7 December 1942. By February 1943, three 'T' hangers were in place. On 1 May 1943 it passed into American hands, some Robin hangars having been added — unusual in this part of Britain.

Throughout 1943 the base was a maintenance depot. An agreement to place RAF Bomber Groups within clutches led on 1 March 1944 to Little Staughton passing to No 8 Group, PFF, Bomber Command. On 1 April a Flight from 7 Squadron and another from 156 Squadron arrived to amalgamate as No 582 Squadron Lancaster-equipped. Next day much of 109 Squadron, PFF, arrived from Marham where runway building was to commence. Mosquitoes of 109 Squadron had been marking invasion targets and undertaking extensive diversion and nuisance raids on Germany. On the night of 4/5 April 1944, 109 Squadron opened Staughton's impressive operational record, with raids on Essen where 'Cookies' were dropped, Cologne, Krefeld, Aachen and Rheinhaussen. That first night was one of the few occasions when an *Oboe* Mosquito failed to return. 'S-Sugar' had crashed in the North Sea.

Lille marshalling yards on the night of 9/10 April 1944 were 582 Squadron's first target, seven crews operating. On 10/11 April they bombed Laon and next night, Aachen. By the end of April they had visited Cologne, Düsseldorf, Karlsruhe, Essen and distant Friedrichshafen, and by the end of April, 582 Squadron had flown 120 sorties and No 109, 190. May was busier, 320 sorties being flown by 109 Squadron and 173 by the Lancasters of 582.

For both squadrons the opening of the Normandy invasion brought a busy night marking coastal batteries. During July 1944, 628 sorties were flown from the station and, in August, 620, an indication of the activity level.

Although losses were lower than at many bomber bases, operations were far from uneventful. On 22/23 May Squadron Leader H.W.B. Heley, flying at 18,000 ft in *JB417:R*, had an incendiary bomb hit his Lancaster's port rudder. Another lodged in the port outer engine before exploding. Heley completed his bombing run, then ordered the crew to prepare to bale out as flames were now trailing behind the wing. A searchlight picked out the bomber and it was seven dangerous minutes before the flames went out. Between Cologne and Gladbach predicted flak hit the Lancaster, yet it still made England.

Near Mepal, Heley switched on his navigation lights because there were many aircraft about. Moments later an intruder attacked the Lancaster from below and astern. With the rear turret out of action, *JB417* was highly vulnerable. Although enemy fire raked the bomber none of the crew was injured. Despite the loss of hydraulics, *JB417* made an emergency landing at Little Staughton after

which the crew discovered that a 500 1b GP bomb had 'hung up'.

The first day raid for 582's Lancasters came on the evening of 30 June 1944 with Villars Bocage as target. No 109 Squadron also took part. Thereafter daylight operations became quite common with 582 Squadron concentrating upon them during the first half of August. Both squadrons took part in tactical bombing raids, including Operation 'Tractable' on 14 August, and Lancasters of 582 Squadron marked for a day raid on the Ghent-Terneuzen Canal on 18 August. In early September 582 Squadron helped to reduce Le Havre's garrison to submission, before Calais and Boulogne received similar treatment . On 3 October the target was West Kapelle with Group Captain P.H. Cribb as Master Bomber in 582's *ND750*.

Rarely did enemy fighters successfully engage Bomber Command's heavies in daylight, but an exception came on 23 December 1944. To attack Cologne's Grimburg marshalling yards seventeen Lancasters of 582 Squadron and a 109 Squadron Mosquito set out in fine weather. Intense flak on the run-in damaged eleven Lancasters, then a mixture of Bf 109s and FW 190s swept through the fighter screen, engaging the bombers over the target. Lancaster 'T-Tommy', flown by Captain Swales, was attacked by eight Bf 109s and a Fw 190 which one of his gunners claimed. Wing Commander Clough's crew fought it out with a Messerschmitt. It was costly for Little Staughton, five Lancasters and a Mosquito failing to return.

Barely had returning Lancasters touched down when four Mosquitoes of 109 Squadron took off to join another 36 attacking Seighburg. A further four were among the 58 despatched to Limburg. During December, 582 Squadron lost seven Lancasters, and by the close of the year, it had flown 1,588 sorties — 147 in December during which 109 Squadron lost five Mosquitoes in the course of 284 sorties.

Nine crews of 582 Squadron participated in the notorious Dresden raid, and the same night six other crews of '582' marked the synthetic oil refinery at Bohlen for 200 bombers of 4 Group and 115 of 6 Group. Chemnitz was twice 582's target at this time. Operations by 109 Squadron included a daylight raid on 6 March when Wesel was bombed, six Mosquitoes leading other 8 Group Mosquitoes.

Offensive operations by Little Staughton's three-Flight squadrons ended on 25 April 1945. Only one of 109 Squadron's aircraft was able to mark the Wachenfels SS Barracks at Berchtesgaden, the rest having technical problems, then came the final fling. Wangerooge's guns were targetted for 25 Lancasters of 582 Squadron and eight crews of 109 Squadron marked.

Both squadrons participated in food drops to the starving Dutch, in early May, and 582 Squadron retrieved PoWs.

Mosquito crews continued training, some of their practice raids being experimentally intercepted by Meteors. The end for 582 Squadron came on 10 September 1945, its Lancasters being flown away to Mepal and Wyton. On the afternoon of 28 September all of 109 Squadron's Mosquitoes left for Upwood, ending Staughton's operational days.

On 24 October 1945 Transport Command took control of the airfield, and Tempsford billetted 300 of its men here from late November. During December 1945 Little Staughton was placed on care & maintenance.

There was considerable discussion as to whether this and Thurleigh could be linked by a long runway for the NAE, but the idea was abandoned although RAE Bedford has had links with Little Staughton. The airfield has seen postwar use by Brooklands Aviation who handled Valettas, Varsities and target-towing Mosquitoes here. A visit in the 1980s reveals assorted light civil aircraft including crop sprayers. The control tower, hangars, dispersals, runways remain, and are easy to view from adjacent roads.

## Lord's Bridge

*TL385545. N of A603, at Comberton/ Barton road junction*

Highly secret-looking, the weird things at Lord's Bridge are not 'radar dishes' but radio telescopes through which discoveries of pulsars and such stellar wonders take place. Nearby is an area where gas bombs were once stored, for 2 and 3 Groups and Lysanders. Despite those, surrounded by a huge bomb dump too, the authorities in 1942 requisitioned a grass field nearby for use as a Relief Landing Ground. Mind you, bombs were stored at many unlikely places during the war, and even in Nissen huts lining public roads and frequently unguarded!

The RLG users, in fine weather, were trainee pilots of 22 EFTS Cambridge who practised forced landings here. At Lord's Bridge one was often confronted by a Tiger Moth suddenly rising from behind the high hedge, and sometimes about to pass over the bomb dumps. To be fair, though, the RLG between 1942 and 1944 was generally in use only when the wind permitted the safest possible activity.

## Mepal

*TL449795. 7 miles W of Ely, on A142. Road crosses site*

Waterbeach became the central station in 33 Base, 3 Group, in 1943. The initial intention was that Mepal, then with two runways, would form the second station, housing 1665 Conversion Unit formed at Waterbeach. The third airfield of the Base was Witchford.

Whilst Mepal had final touches put to it in the spring of 1943, 1665 CU made use of Great Ashfield. When the time came to move the unit to Mepal it had been decided that Waterbeach would again become an operational station. To use Mepal for training was illogical, and it became on 25 June 1943 a sub-station

**Above** *Several Cambridgeshire airfields were built on former flying sites. This blimp was photographed at Sutton near Mepal on 23 October 1913 (Cambridgeshire Collection).*

**Below** *Lancasters of 'C' Flight, 75 (NZ) Squadron, setting off from Mepal.*

**Above** *Summer '83 and Lindsay Walton's Corsair poses before a Duxford show crowd and the B-29.*

**Below** *Rare indeed, two Jetstream pilot trainers of 5 FTS Oakington, October 1974.*

**Above** *Varsity WJ921 taxying by Oakington's control tower and a 'J' Type hangar, May 1972.*

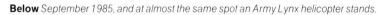

**Below** *September 1985, and at almost the same spot an Army Lynx helicopter stands.*

**Above** XG260, a 54 Squadron Hunter FGA 9 (Interim) on the ASP at Waterbeach moments before the station closed to operational flying in 1963.

**Below** *Civilian flying in Cambridgeshire has been concentrated at Cambridge. In wartime, however, numerous impressed aircraft were also resident including DH Hornet Moth G-AELO (then AW118).*

**Above** *Most colourful of Canberras, TT 18 WJ682 of Wyton's 100 Squadron.*

**Below** *In recent years Wyton held the RAF's two longest serving aircraft, a de Havilland Devon and Canberra T 17 WD955 of 360 Squadron.*

*In immediate post-war markings, Lancaster AA:P–ND974 of 75 Squadron at Mepal.*

of Waterbeach to accommodate 24 aircraft. Newmarket was unsuitable for heavily laden Lancasters and, in the general re-arrangement of bomber stations, 75 (RNZAF) Squadron left Newmarket on 28 June 1943 and brought its Stirlings to Mepal. No 75 was a three-Flight squadron and busily operating at the time, mounting its first operation from the new station on 3 July against Cologne. Thereafter the Stirlings took part in many 3 Group operations, flew a large number of mining sorties and dropped supplies to the French.

During March 1944 the squadron re-equipped with Lancaster I/IIIs, first operating them in April whilst Stirlings were still in use. Main Force raids followed and at the end of the war 75 Squadron dropped food to the Dutch.

Hurried movement of 75 Squadron to Spilsby in July 1945 was partly brought about by the arrival of Transport Command at Oakington, and rapid wind-down of other squadrons and bases. In July 1945 44 Squadron's Lancasters arrived from 5 Group and 7 Squadron from Oakington, forming part of Tiger Force for the Far East. No 44 left in August, replaced by 49 Squadron, the former having gone to Mildenhall to continue Lincoln trials. Nos 7 and 49 remained at Mepal until July 1946 when the station was put on care & maintenance.

To all intents and purposes Mepal passed away until 1958 when the site, still in official hands, took on a completely new look. Buildings were placed in the centre of the airfield, which had only been the site of two 'T' hangars and a few huts close to Mepal village. Now, by the Chatteris road which opened after the war, a high fence was erected within which were placed three launching sites and associated buildings for 113 Squadron's Thor missiles. The Thors under 3 Group remained here until 1963, having been brought to high readiness during the Cuban missile crisis.

After the Thors were withdrawn Mepal fell into decay and reverted to farming. Jardin's have converted a hangar into

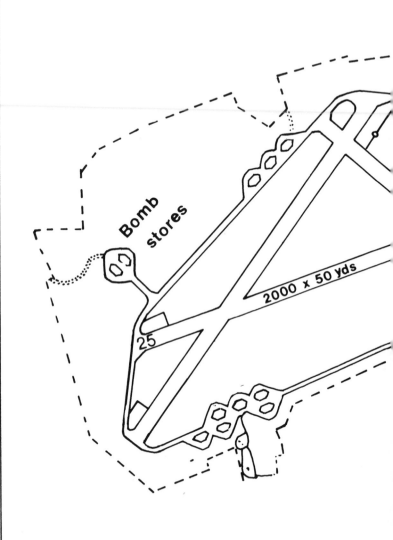

Bomb stores

2000 x 50 yds

25

1944 Mepal has two 'T2' and a 'B1' hangars, 36 Loop hardstandings and many small domestic sites to the east.

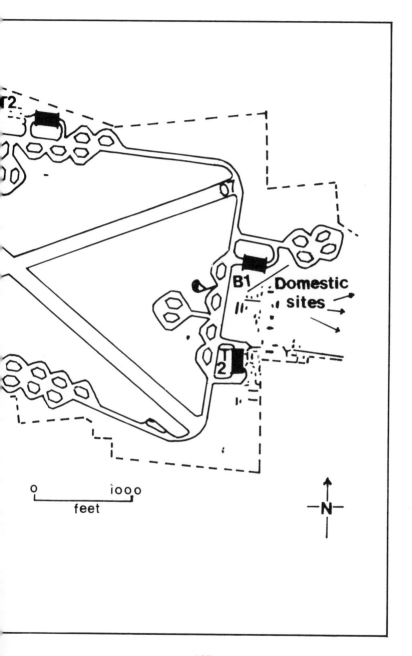

their corrugated paper factory. The taxi track largely remains, also the control tower and some blast walls. The airfield is best viewed from the road which crosses it.

# Molesworth

*TL008775. E of Thrapston, best seen from B660 near Old Weston, N of A604*
Molesworth! A place of delight for any protestor. Mention the magic words 'Hell's Angels' — a group which fought gallantly from here, laying down many lives for our freedom, in a manner far more likely to secure it than the antics of some today — and the odds are that it will mean precisely nothing. All history proves beyond any doubt that freedom is for those, and only those, with the courage, means and determination to retain it. Whether the storage of cruise missiles at Molesworth is a good idea, or whether we all would be better safeguarded by the stationing of B-1s or 'Stealth' bombers with their accompanying noise, are arguable points. What is not in doubt is that Molesworth has an interesting and unusual history.

Planned in 1939, it was built in 1940-1 as a bomber base with a single 'J' Type hangar, with associated services close by in serried rows. An RAF opening party arrived on 15 May 1941. It was intended to be an RAF Liberator base but, on 15 November 1941, a new Australian squadron, No 460, formed here armed with American-engined Wellington IVs. Kimbolton was already Molesworth's satellite and indeed, the first Wellington for 460 Squadron placed itself there on 29 November. No operations were flown before 460 Squadron left for Breighton on 5 January 1942. Molesworth's first association with operational flying came three days later when a Wellington of 9 Squadron landed there from operations.

Molesworth's next occupants were crews of 159 Squadron who had learnt to use Liberators when at Polebrook. Their 'aircraftless' stay was brief for, on 12 February 1942, they left. Next day thir-teen Blenheims of 'A' and 'B' Flights, 17 OTU, came because Upwood was unserviceable. Some returned home on 17 February, the remainder in March.

On 27 February 1942, General Ira Eaker brought along four of his staff to view the station for possible American use. Major improvements followed, including runway extensions and additional dispersal areas. More accommodation was built and two 'T2' hangars added. Another unexpected interlude began on 13 March 1942, thirteen Master IIIs of 5 SFTS Ternhill arriving for a month's stay along with three Hurricanes.

In May 1942 preparations raced ahead for the establishment of No 2 Depot. On 10 May the station was placed on care & maintenance then, during the evening of 12 May, foreigners arrived under the command of Major M.C. Carpenter. Throughout May more Americans moved in, and in early June ground personnel of the 31st Fighter Group were briefly here, and in mid-June some of the 5th Photographic Squadron. The greatest excitement greeted the arrival, on 9 June 1942, of the 15th Bomb Squadron here to operate, and which that day received a couple of Boston IIIs and a helpless Tiger Moth.

Crews of the 15th had come to discover how to use Douglas A-20s as night fighter/interdictors. The aircraft had been switched to day bombing and the Americans decided to see it perform such duty. Having no operational aircraft of its own, the 15th borrowed Boston IIIs from No 226 Squadron RAF, Swanton Morley. Crewing one of their aircraft on 29 June, a Molesworth team, headed by Captain Kegelman, carried out the first USAAF bombing raid on a European target, the Hazebrouck marshalling yards. Some Bostons were acquired in July and decorated in US insignia. More personnel arrived on 14 July; their crusade, the effective operation of their vaunted Flying Fortress.

Of the date of the arrival of the first B-

17F Fortress there seems uncertainty, but I first recorded one there on 5 August. The 5th Photographic Reconnaissance Squadron left on 10 September and the 15th Bomb Squadron three days later. All was now clear for the arrival of the 303rd Bomb Group which left Biggs Field, Texas, and began moving in on 12 September after a five-day Atlantic crossing in the *Queen Mary*. By the end of the war in Europe the 303rd was to fly more operational sorties (10,721) than any other 8th AF Group, and in the course of 364 operations.

On 17 November 1942, sixteen B-17Fs of the 303rd flew their first operation, the target being U-boat pens at St Nazaire. Bombs were brought back for the target was thickly cloud-clad. Next day they tried for La Pallice, bombed — and discovered that they had hit the previous day's target! A few days later they redeemed themselves as the only Group to bomb Lorient during a difficult operation.

Committed to operations, 'Hell's Angels' joined in most major attacks by the 8th AF including the Wilhelmshaven raid of 27 January 1943, when the 8th AF introduced itself to the residents of the Fatherland. They visted Hamm on 2 February.

It was 18 March 1943 when the courage suddenly demanded on operations was dramatically displayed. Lieutenant Jack W. Mathis was bombardier in *The Duchess*, a B-17F of the 358th bomb Squadron. As the aircraft ran in on target a shell burst close to the nose, hurling Mathis back into the fuselage. Horrifically wounded, he summoned the courage to drag himself back to the bombsight and released the bomb load before he died. He was posthumously awarded the Medal of Honor.

Raids took the group to well-known targets including Huls synthetic rubber factory, Bremen's shipyards, Hamburg, Frankfurt and Schweinfurt. Many targets in France were attacked both prior to, and following, D-Day, by which time another

member of the 303rd had been awarded the Medal of Honor. Technical Sergeant Forrest L. Vosler, also of the 358th, was aboard *Jersey Bounce Jr* and ordered to bomb Bremen on 20 December 1943. Heavy flak was encountered after which German fighters pestered the damaged Fortress, Vosler, seriously wounded, continued with his task, aiding defence of the B-17. Eventually the aircraft ditched in the Channel. Despite terrible wounds, Vosler held another member of the crew aboard until both were transferred to a dinghy. After ten months treatment Vosler was invalided out of the Air Force.

As well as courageous men, Molesworth was the base of famous Fortresses. One was the B-17F *Hell's Angels, 41-24577* of the 358th Bomb Squadron, the first B-17 to complete 25 operational sorties over Europe. Another was *Knockout Dropper*, the first B-17 to manage 75 sorties — the equivalent to three crew tours. As *41-24605* it had arrived in Britain in October 1942, joined the 359th Bomb Squadron, became *BN-R* and brought its crew home each time without any being wounded. During the Oschersleben raid of 11 January 1944, when the 303rd was leading the 1st Air Division, ten B-17s were shot down by intense fighter onslaught. The courage of all won the group a Distinguished Unit Citation. Molesworth remains a place at which to remember courage.

The 303rd, making its final operation on 25 April 1945, bombed Pilsen in Czechoslovakia. In early June the Group moved to North Africa. The RAF repossessed Molesworth on 1 July 1945. Affinity to things American continued, Nos 441 and 442 Canadian squadrons bringing Mustang IIIs and IVs on 16 July. On 27 July 1945 a rare sight and sound arrived as Meteor IIIs of 1335 Conversion Unit came in from Colerne. They were to convert piston-engined fighter squadrons to jet aircraft. Both Canadian squadrons disbanded on 10 August, and were replaced by 234 Squadron.

On 7 September 1945, Mustang IVs of

19 Squadron moved in, then in March 1946, Spitfire XVIs replaced the Mustangs and the squadron left on 28 June. Spitfire IXs of 129 Squadron had arrived from Brussels on 9 November 1945 and left for Hutton Cranswick on 3 December. No 124 Squadron, here from August to 6 October 1945, flew Meteor IIIs. In late October 1945, 222 Squadron came from Weston Zoyland to convert to Meteors.

At about 01:00 on 20 November a guardroom Corporal heard an unexpected roar. A Meteor was making an unauthorized flight. The roll call showed Pilot Officer J.E. Adam missing, along with *EE316*. The general hullabaloo brought the special investigation branch along and 12 Group held a court of inquiry.

On 11 December 1945, 222 Squadron left for Exeter. Following a winter break, 234 Squadron came in mid-February to convert to Meteors, leaving for Boxted in March. Between September and October 1946, Tempest IIs of 54 Squadron were based here, then the station was placed on care & maintenance.

Molesworth's very open approaches and good weather record led to it being improved, and re-opened for the USAF in July 1951. A long runway was laid, superimposed upon the conventional three-runway site. The base opened for flying in February 1954. Unusual were the new occupants for, when the 582nd Air Resupply Group arrived late that month, it brought a dozen B-29As, four Grumman SA-16A amphibians, three C-119Cs and a C-47. The B-29s role hidden under security wraps was said to include 'supply dropping and giving assistance to crews who had come down in difficult terrain'. A few B-45s of the 47th Bomb Wing briefly were at Molesworth in mid-1956 whilst their home base had runway repairs.

On 25 October 1956 the 582nd ARG dissolved into a new 42nd Troop Carrier Squadron (Medium) directly controlled by USAFE through HQ 3rd AF. Gone the B-29s, their places taken by C-119Cs, a few C-54s, C-47s and SA-16As merely switching owners. This unit's stay was brief for, on 31 May 1957, it came under Alconbury's control before being deactivated there on 8 December 1957. Transport aircraft continued to call for some time because Molesworth was a supply depot for the USAF as well as a reserve airfield. A few Boeing WB-50s

*A few B-29s operated from Molesworth in the 1950s including 461754 photographed in 1956.*

made use of Molesworth in the late 1950s.

Using Molesworth as a missile base has a touch of irony. Immediate post-war plans called for the retention of Polebrook as a bomber station. In 1947 it was rejected in favour of Molesworth, Air Ministry tenure of Polebrook being sufficient for the later accommodation of a trio of Thor ballistic missiles. Now the 1980s have seen Molesworth surrender any possibility of further use as an airfield. The Secure Area in which the Tomahawk missiles are to be stored, within the 550th TAM's GLCM Alert and Maintenance Area, straddles what once was the long runway. Molesworth is officially stated to be the intended home for four Flights each capable of launching sixteen missiles. Completion date for the project is 1988.

All warfare is immoral, all weapons are designed to contain and usually to kill. None differentiate between civilian and military targets and in modern war a case could probably, cynically, be made out for entire nations being part of any war effort. According to its own proud boasting the USSR has dedicated itself to overtake by any means available the Free societies of the West – one Russian leader actually told myself and a few others of this intent as he stood by the control tower at Marham. The establishment of NATO came within months of the USSR having established the means to subdue our freedom, and there is no question that 1950 all but saw the end of all that we cherish. The movement to Britain of substantial American forces immediately altered that situation.

If you stand outside Molesworth's perimeter to protest you will surely do so with deep conviction. What has, however, to be asked is 'Upon what certain knowledge do you base your conviction that there is no need for a nuclear deterrent?' A riding question must also be 'When did you last have access to the necessary daily top secret intelligence summaries which are essential reading before the formulation of any attitude has any worthwhile validity?'

# Oakington

*TL409655. 2 miles N of A604, 6 miles NW of Cambridge*

'Stirling'. The very name is synonymous with Oakington. It also means '7 Squad-

*The Grose Monoplane, a 1910-style Oakington 'flier'* (Cambridgeshire Collection).

ron' which, from late 1940 to the end of the war, fought valiantly from the station by night and day.

The present airfield is not the first at Oakington, for in 1910 attempts were there made to fly the Grose Monoplane, but building of RAF Oakington commenced in 1939, hence the two Type 'J' hangars. The unfinished station opened on 1 July 1940, Wing Commander L.B. Duggen taking command at a time when many personnel were accommodated in tents. No 218 Squadron's Blenheim IVs moved in on 14 July 1940 and were dispersed on the south side. They commenced daylight operations against Dutch airfields on 19 August.

The most memorable event of summer 1940 came on 19 September. Blenheims were making mock attacks on the airfield for the benefit of army defenders. Suddenly a 'Blenheim' unexpectedly made an approach and belly landed, whilst two Hurricanes of 17 Squadron zoomed overhead. In fact it was not a Blenheim, it was Ju 88a *7A+FM*, Werk Nr 0362, of 4(F)/121, packed with cameras and which had engine trouble. Lieutenant Helmut Knab and his crew were captured.

The arrival of the Ju 88 was fortuitous. It contained excellent cameras of which the station soon made use. On 16 November 1940 No 3 Photographic Reconnaissance Unit formed here under Bomber Command for damage assessment duties. It brought in some astonishing Spitfires specially modified for the task and painted in a variety of colours including the customary grey-blue but also white, and even pink to tone with evening skies at high altitudes. Those German cameras proved very useful now. The first Spitfire operation was flown on 29 November 1940, to photograph Cologne, after which 3 PRU flew many sorties and acquired some Wellingtons for night photography by the aid of high-powered flash bulbs.

It was the arrival of 7 Squadron on 29 October 1940 that heralded the Stirling era. The squadron took some time fully to move in. Such was the state of the Stirling programme that in November they had only two aircraft here. There was nothing basically wrong with the aircraft apart from low-powered engines, but an assortment of small faults added up to give it a protracted teething period. It brought chagrin to the squadron to find that the aircraft would easily fit the hangars, yet span had been reduced in the project stage to allow indoor servicing of a number of aircraft simultaneously.

By then Oakington had become the centre of a quite different 'storm'. Lord Beaverbrook in November 1940 pointed out to the Air Ministry that forthcoming heavy bombers needed concrete runways 1,500 yd in length, whereas the few existing were only 1,000 yd long. Furthermore, and with Oakington principally in mind, he was pointing out that winter conditions were causing unsettled turf on new airfields to be ruined once aircraft were flying from such stations. He also suggested tarmac runways in place of concrete. The Air Ministry then decided that airfield runways should be on the scale of 1 × 1,400 yd and 2 × 1,100 yd — for new airfields and satellites.

The Ministry of Aircraft Production had raised the question of why Oakington with a grass surface was chosen for Stirlings. The Air Ministry stated that the choice came about after considering weather, approaches, geography and advice indicating that the airfield's soil and drainage features were satisfactory. It was believed that by autumn 1941 the turf would have settled well enough to permit full scale operations. Bomber Command had moved the Stirlings from 4 Group, and it transpired that the Command was not in favour of runways because they could not readily be camouflaged. The new heavy bombers would thus be at risk from intruders airfields with hard runways. Not until 4 January 1941 did Bomber Command at last express any wish for runways at its stations.

*Autumn 1941 and Stirling* MG:D-W7436 *(lost during the famous Brest raid of 18 December 1941) is prepared for operations.*

Only five airfields in Britain had runways laid before the war, mainly on account of the cost. The only reason for having any was due to the fear of hard wear on unstable surfaces, and even in February 1941 Bomber Command only wished for runways at Stradishall. For new airfields runways provided hard surfaces quickly whereas grass areas took many months to establish, and involved much continuous labour.

By April 1941 one hundred new airfields were being built with runways, the latter by then being provided at another twenty. A further fifty airfields with runways were being planned, twenty of which were about to be started.

Bomber Command had listed Oakington as only seventh on a list for runway building. A flurry of official activity brought important visitors to Oakington, mostly by road because often it was unserviceable.

Stirlings frequently took off lightly loaded and bombed up at Wyton. Not for long could that continue, because conditions were just as awful at that station. Grass-surfaced airfields were, simply, unsuitable for heavy aircraft.

January 1941 found Oakington's surface in a terrible state, a mass of mud on the days when the ice thawed, a slippery morass when water froze; and it snowed often. Indeed, it was so cold that there was a rum ration 'to approved personnel'. Occasionally a Stirling made a flight, to the delight of the locals, and on 19 February, long before the aircraft was ready to fight, three Stirlings made the first raid, against Rotterdam.

Oakington already had its satellite at Bourn and on 7 February 1941 personnel were sent there for ground defence duties. Equipment had already arrived at Oakington for the handling of 2,000 lb

*Aerial view of 1942 Oakington* (RAF Museum).

bombs, the largest weapons the Stirling could carry.

The airfield had been declared unsuitable for Spitfires on 22 January and operations were at once switched to Alconbury, Wellingtons flying their first night sorties from Newmarket on 5 and 6 February. On 25 February the 50th Spitfire sortie was flown. No 3 PRU usually held about six Spitfires and flew a large number of sorties with them before disbanding late in July 1941. By then Oakington's Stirlings were hitting the headlines, particularly with their daylight raids, but throughout 1941 the aircraft remained few in number. Oakington's runways were completed in the spring. The highlight of the year was a day raid on Brest on 18 December.

On 30 May 1942 word passed around among the villagers at Oakington that 1,000 bombers would operate that night, against Cologne. It seemed impossible. This was 7 Squadron's biggest raid yet and in addition to its nineteen Stirlings, twelve Wellingtons of 101 Squadron

operated from Bourn under Oakington's control. That squadron had arrived at Oakington in June 1941 flying Wellington Ics and moved to Bourn on 11 February 1942. No 23 OTU placed five Wellington Ics at each of these stations for the '1,000 bomber' raids. Of the whole force of 41 aircraft, 33 claimed successful attacks.

In August 1942, 7 Squadron switched to the pathfinding role. Now, the Stirlings often carried flare loads mixed with some high explosive, and back-up primary markers. A gradual switch to flares/target indicators and large incendiary loads came, particularly during the Battle of the Ruhr in 1943. On 11 May 1943, 7 Squadron began to re-equip with Lancasters which took over the operational role completely on 12 August 1943. Bomb loads immediately increased. No 7 Squadron made a great contribution to the bomber offensive, being a three-Flight squadron. It was busy during the Battle of Berlin, and sustained a constant campaign including marking gun batteries on 5/6 June 1944.

*Distinguished all-black Mosquito B IV AZ:F–DZ518 of 627 Squadron on an Oakington dispersal in January 1944* (Douglas Garton, via P.H.T. Green).

Early in 1943 Bellman hangars were erected. Their purpose was to provide a home for an entirely different phase in Oakington's history for here, on 1 April 1943, No 1409 Meteorological Flight formed with eight Mosquito IVs from 521 Squadron. Its task was to seek out weather patterns for the whole of Bomber Command, PAMPA flights beginning on 2 April. In May 1943 it began to use Mosquito IXs and by the time it moved to Wyton on 8 January 1944 was fully equipped with that type.

No 627 Mosquito squadron, an off-shoot of 139 Squadron, formed on 12 November 1943 at Oakington for bombing operations which commenced on the 24th when *DZ615* bombed Berlin, target for nearly 100 of the 291 sorties flown by the squadron from Oakington for the total loss of three aircraft. Four of its Mosquito IVs were each able to carry a 4,0000-lb bomb. In mid-April 1944 the squadron moved to Woodhall Spa, joining 5 Group as marker squadron for 'The Dam Busters'.

On 24 April 1944 Mosquito IXs/XVIs of 571 Squadron completed moving in from Downham Market and later that day had two aircraft attacking Düsseldorf. The squadron operated mainly at night in 8 Group's LNSF despatching 2,520 sorties, the last against Grossenbrode on 26 April 1945. Only nine Mosquitoes failed to return from operations. Oakington's combination of Lancasters and Mosquitoes was an example of the most efficient and effective bomber team the Allies possessed.

No 571 Squadron left for Warboys on 20 July then abruptly on 24 July 1945 No 7 Squadron moved to Mepal, and Transport Command immediately seized Oakington. The first Liberator of 206 Squadron and still in Coastal Command colours arrived, and so rapid was the change-over that next day two Liberators commenced training flights to India before their squadron had completely moved in from Leuchars. No 86 Squadron's Liberators began arriving on 1 August. Both squadrons airlifted Indian troops to their homeland, and on returning brought home British troops for demobilization. Such flights lasted into 1946, then on 25 April both squadrons disbanded.

The start of May 1946 witnessed the arrival of Avro Yorks of 242 Squadron which contributed to trunk route services mainly to the Far East. At the end of November 1947 the squadron left for Abingdon from where in August 1947 238 Squadron had brought Dakotas to Oakington. On 24 November 1947 Nos 27 and 30 Squadrons re-formed here with Dakotas at which time more, of 46 Squadron, moved in. Being part of the airborne assault force they also held a pool of Horsa gliders.

July 1948's commencement of the blockade of Berlin caused the station to despatch most of its Dakotas to Germany to participate in the Berlin Airlift. No 238 Squadron was re-numbered 10 Squadron on 5 November 1948 and spent much of 1949 at Lübeck from where it returned in September to dis-

band at Oakington on 20 February 1950. No 18 Squadron was also briefly at Oakington in 1949 before settling at Waterbeach in October. No 46 Squadron disbanded here on 20 February 1950 and 27 Squadron disbanded later that year.

February 1950 saw the arrival of 24 Squadron from Waterbeach. Dakotas and Yorks equipped this squadron whose first operational sortie from Oakington was to Zurich, via Northolt, by Dakota *KJ994* on 25 February. Transport of VIPs remained its task until the last week of November 1950 when its twin-engined aircraft were transfered to 30 Squadron. The remainder of the squadron left for Lyneham on the 27th and conversion to Hastings transports.

During November 1950 Transport Command relinquished its hold on Oakington which passed into 23 Group, Training Command, which moved No 1 Flying Training School and its Harvards to the station. Their noisy stay extended to October 1951, then No 206 Advanced Flying School took over on 29th, its Main

*Vampire trainers, daily Oakington sight of the 1950s.*

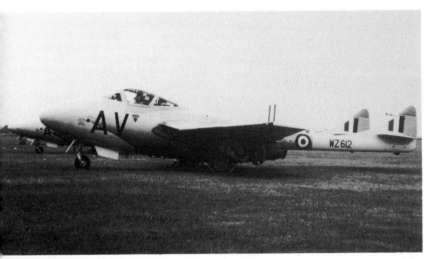

Party arriving from North Luffenham and the defunct 102 FRS on 7 November — the day when 206 AFS became an effective unit. Its first course opened on 5 December, students commencing flying on Meteor T7s then progressing to refurbished Meteor IIIs. Intensity of activity was soon very high both here and at the RLG, Gravley. Indeed, one day in January 1953 produced an amazing 612 movements, although the daily average was about 200 'rollers' at Oakington and 100 at Gravley.

No 206 AFS wound down during May 1954, but there was not much evidence of change at Oakington for on 1 June 1954 the unit's remains were absorbed by a new No 5 Flying Training School soon flying Meteor T7s and Vampire 5s and 9s. September 1959 saw the replacement of the T7s by Vampire T11s as the Provost-Vampire training programme for new pilots was brought fully into play. Within a few weeks the T7s were back — needed for the training of long-legged pilots!

In 1963 Varsities came into use as the school switched to training pilots for multi-engined aircraft. Again the flying was of high intensity, engines of some of the aircraft running non-stop from 08:00 to 17:00 hours. By the mid-1970s the Varsity was an aged affair quite unsuited to airways training, an essential feature of the syllabus. Late summer 1974 saw the introduction of Jetstreams, but their stay was brief for by the end of the year No 5 FTS was no more, its task taken over by Finningley.

The last official RAF flight from Oakington was made by Wessex XT606 on 7 May 1975, but flying here was far from over. The camp was one of a number passed to the Army for accommodating troops brought back to Britain as a result of the pull-back from Germany, Malta and East of Suez. Initially the Green Jackets moved in, then early in 1976 came the arrival from Colchester of Scouts and Gazelle helicopters of No 657 Squadron. In 1984 — by which time the

2nd Battalion, The Queen's Regiment had moved in — the squadron replaced its Scout element with Lynx helicopters which, using TOW missiles, have primarily an anti-tank role. Whilst its helicopters remain at Oakington, the squadron personnel take their share of garrison duty in the Falklands.

Beavers are the most likely fixed-wing machines to be seen using Oakington nowadays; most of its runway has gone and patches of trees and bushes have been planted on the landing ground as much for ecological purposes as for infantry training.

# Peterborough
## (Westwood)

*TF165002. 2 miles NW of the city, now an industrial estate*

On 2 December 1935, No 7 SFTS formed at Peterborough, a most unusual station, to which the previous month seventeen Hawker Hart (T)s (*K4983-4999*) had been posted. For company they had Avro Tutors, Furies, Audaxes received in February 1936 and Harts two months later. A boost came on 17 January 1939 when the first Oxford arrived.

Major upheaval in the programme took place between May and July 1939, the station being at half strength as it switched to training FAA pilots. The flying course was reduced to four months at the outbreak of war. Further alteration came during October 1939 when the school switched to single-engine aircraft courses and the Oxfords left. Nominal strength was 24 Hart (T)s and eight Audaxes in the Initial Training Squadron with 24 Audaxes and eight Hart (T)s in the Advanced Training Squadron. January 1940 brought a new shape when the establishment altered to include 29 Battle Trainers, 34 Hart (T)s and 21 Audaxes. In summer of 1940, 7 SFTS was ordered to hold in readiness twelve Harts for bombing duty within Plan 'Banquet' for which the operational base would have been Stradishall.

During July 1940 7 SFTS started using Sibson RLG for night flying training, short-lived because the school was ordered in August to prepare to leave for Canada, one of seven units told to make the Atlantic crossing. The first echelon left on 29 August 1940 to join no 31 SFTS the last in January 1941.

Peterborough was switched to 50 Group on 20 December 1941 and 13 EFTS moved in from White Waltham by 11 January 1941 with a swarm of Tiger Moths. Their stay was, however, brief for, on 31 May, 72 'Tigers' flew to Booker to form the basis of 21 EFTS. On 1 June No 25 (Polish) EFTS formed in 21 Group at Peterborough and also used Sibson. Again its stay was short and, with only 57 of the scheduled Tiger Moths in hand, it left for Hucknall in mid-July 1941. Yet another Tiger Moth school replaced the

Poles — No 17 EFTS which arrived from North Luffenham on 15 July 1941 and remained at Peterborough until disbandment on 1 June 1942.

Replacement came the same day with the birth of 7 (Pilots) Advanced Flying Unit. Miles Master I and II-equipped, this refresher school expanded fast soon placing two Flights permanently at Sibson. By April 1943 it had up to 130 Masters (mainly MK IIs) and four Ansons. The pupil population similarly increased from ninety to 211 pilots. A further two Flights then formed. To answer the need for night fighter pilots, night flying commenced at King's Cliffe on 25 June 1943, the three stations now in use allowing a constant pupil population of 150 to be flying. King's Cliffe, though, was required for operational flying and 7 (P) AFU vacated it in July.

*BEA helicopters including Bell 47s were Peterborough-based in the 1950s for the experimental East Anglia postal service.*

A visit to Peterborough afforded a sky packed with Masters of various types and in conflicting markings, a state which continued into 1944. A Flight of some fifteen Hurricanes was added to the unit in March 1944, at the time when command passed to the well-known Wing Commander J. M. Foxley-Norris.

In August 1944 the use of Sibson largely ended. On 8 August, Sutton Bridge came into 7 (P) AFU hands as its satellite where, since June 1944, the unit had been night flying. No 7 (P) AFU was reorganized into two Advanced Flights, a Gunnery Flight and two Battle Flights. At Sutton Bridge 22 Oxfords arrived during September 1944 for the opening of a new 7 (P) AFU, soon a fully fledged and new SFTS, still under Peterborough's control. As a result of the change, eight Hurricanes were promptly taken from Peterborough and plans were made to retire the 95 Masters on roll and replace them, in the spring of 1945, with Harvards (which came into use in May 1945) and supplement those with a few aged Spitfire IIs.

At Peterborough, 7 SFTS was reborn on 21 December 1944. The training pattern called for one-third of the pilots to pass out as single-engined trained. Many pupils were French for their newly formed Air Force. Instruction by the spring was undertaken using 47 Oxfords, 29 Harvards and four Ansons. No 1 French Course of 32 pilots passed out in February while the Masters were still in use and as the Spitfires were being removed. Night flying was undertaken at Wittering.

In June 1945, with Wittering and Sutton Bridge still in use, the last Master on strength, AZ497, was ready to leave. In the immediate post-war period, training continued with Oxfords and Harvards until, on 4 April 1946, the main party of 7 SFTS left for Kirton there to join 5 SFTS, after which Peterborough was put on to care & maintenance. Apart from its use for BEA helicopters, the airfield saw very little post-war use and has now been overtaken by an industrial estate.

# Sibson

*TL095960. 7 miles SW of Peterborough, by B671, S of Wansford*

Sibson's grassland became an aerodrome by addition of a few tents, and portable flares for night flying. Use as Peterborough's RLG began in July 1940 and it was bombed the following month. At this time it was being used for the training of naval pilots, using Harts and Audaxes.

In January 1941, Sibson was transferred to Cranfield control. Oxford pilots trained here until 14 SFTS left in June. On 15 June 1941, No 2 CFS Church Lawford acquired the use of Sibson for Tutors and Oxfords, which flew from here until mid-January 1942. This unit shared Sibson with Peterborough which regained control in July 1941. Use had been made of it by Tiger Moths of 25 EFTS, replaced by others of 17 EFTS which did circuit training here until the school disbanded on 1 June 1942.

That date coincided with the formation of 7 (P) AFU at Peterborough, a unit which equipped itself with many Master IIs. Controlled by 21 Group, it placed its 'A' and 'B' Flights at Sibson on a permanent basis in August 1942. By mid-1943 there were two day-flying Flights and a night-flying Flight at Sibson. Increased flying brought about improvements and enlargements to a once spartan site which were needed to cope with its increased use.

Throughout 1943 and into the summer of 1944, the Master IIs of 7 (P) AFU were ever active in the area and, occasionally, Hurricanes of the same unit. There was intense operational flying around Sibson. This and the amount of mixed flying from Wittering was hardly condusive to pilot training. Accordingly, 7 (P) AFU relinquished its hold on Sibson in August 1944, moving to long established Sutton Bridge.

Some flying continued at Sibson to the end of 1944 then, early in 1945, it was placed on care & maintenance. Sibson closed on 21 May 1946 and was placed under care & maintenance in the hands of Flying Training Command. Fighter Command took over the station on 8 July 1946 before it closed again on 1 October 1946.

Since the 1960s Sibson has been a centre for civilian flying and has become the Peterborough Parachute Centre.

# Snailwell

*TL655675. Off A142, to right, just N of Newmarket*

Snailwell opened in March 1941. On 1 April Lysanders of 268 Squadron moved in from Westley — too small for Tomahawks with which 268 Squadron re-equipped in May. Snailwell, conceived as Duxford's second satellite opened on 1 May. The station instead slipped into Army Co-operation Command hands. Three months later and although attached to Duxford, a Station HQ opened here allowing Snailwell to function independently.

Throughout 1941 Snailwell echoed to the tinny note of Lysanders and high pitched call of Tomahawks as many Army exercises were mounted. Prior to 14 February 1942, 268 Squadron engaged in no more than one day's operational flying. Then came detachments to Ibsley, Hampshire, whence the Tomahawks flew Channel Patrols alongside 501 Squadron's Spitfires.

In March 1942 Typhoons of 56 Squadron arrived from Duxford. Within a few days they were joined by Mustangs Is for 268 Squadron which on 29 June despatched its first two *Lagoons*, searches for shipping between Texel and the Hook, many of which were to be flown from Snailwell. At this time '268' was attached to 2 Corps, Eastern Command.

The Typhoons soon started practising low-level *Rhubarbs* under Squadron Leader 'Cocky' Dundas and, from 29 May, detached Flights were placed at Manston and West Hampnett to face low-flying fighter-bombers. On 20 June 1942 '56' operated from Duxford in the first Typhoon Wing sweep over the Boulogne-Mardyck area, landing back at Snailwell. Similar operations followed then, on 19 August, 56 Squadron participated from West Malling in the Dieppe operation facing Fw 190s for the first time. On 24 August the squadron moved to Matlaske.

No 168 Tomahawk Squadron reformed here on 15 June 1942 from 268 Squadron and also used Bottisham. During August 1942 Whirlwinds of 137 Squadron — briefly here in March for Army support training — returned to Snailwell from where in September the Squadron Commander first sampled the Whirlwind as a fighter-bomber before on 12 September '137' moved to Manston.

Blenheims of 614 Squadron arrived for a short stay then on 16 October the Americans placed P-39 Airacobras of the 347th Fighter Squadron here. They left for King's Cliffe on 8 December, their place quickly being filled by the first 'Bomphoon' squadron, No 181, whose 'A' Flight left for Ludham and the commencement of operations in February 1943.

Snailwell was by then a very active station with 268 Squadron's Mustang Is operating *Lagoons* when the weather allowed or the need dictated. On 11 January 1943 the squadron supported the first RAF Mitchell raid. Fw 190s were engaged and one destroyed for the loss of a Mustang. During another memorable operation seven Mustangs on 12 February strafed the SS barracks at Amersfoort then destroyed a Do 217 landing at Soesterberg. The 'Bomphoons' moved to Gravesend on 24 March, their place being taken by 170 Squadron's Mustangs whose ground crews were ferried in aboard Horsa gliders. Shortly after, a Glider MU HQ was established at Snailwell, but no gliders were ever held here. No 170 Squadron was meanwhile attached to the local Guard's Armoured Division before being posted to Odiham on 26 June 1943.

Early in May 1943 309 (Polish) Squadron brought in Mustang Is and between 28 June and October 1943 flew *Lagoons*. On 4 October they flew an eight-aircraft *Distil* operation off Denmark, trying to shoot down minesweeping Ju 52s.

Operating alongside 309 was 613 Squadron whose Mustangs began *Lagoons* in mid-July. They operated almost daily until 8 October 1943, their role being threefold: reconnaissance for enemy ships, some PR and a few ASR Walrus escorts, all undertaken under 12 Group, which took control of the station when Army Co-operation Command disbanded at the end of May 1943. No 613 Squadron left in mid-November when 309 Squadron resumed *Lagoons* which continued until January 1944.

Close association with Duxford and AFDU briefly brought No 1426 Enemy Aircraft Flight here with its assortment of German aircraft in July 1943. The famous He 111, AW177, was operating from Snailwell when it crashed on the runway at Polebrook on 10 November 1943. That autumn also saw detachments of 116 and 288 Squadrons using the station for radar calibration and AA support duties. An abrupt change came about on 8 February 1944. No 309 Squadron had flown its last *Lagoon* on this day and the squadron began to equip with Hurricane II/IVs, worked up and moved north on 23 April. As a pointer to the future 417 Repair & Salvage Unit formed here on 1 January 1944, and on 1 March left for Lasham and an important role in the invasion.

No 527 Squadron flying six Blenheim IVs, eight Hurricanes and four DH Hornet Moths arrived from Castle Camps on 28 February 1944 and stayed until late in April flying calibration sorties. Then the station was relieved of aircraft.

On 7 May the 41st Base Complement Squadron, USAAF, moved in, the 33rd and 41st MR Squadrons arriving soon after, and having a few A-20Gs here in summer. The Americans stayed until autumn, the RAF having closed its SHQ on 15 July.

During October 1944 the RAF (Belgian) Initial Training School moved into Snailwell, its purpose to train air and ground crews for the post-war Belgian Air Force. Tiger Moths and Master IIs arrived in February 1945 and flying training commenced. Personnel were accommodated both at this station and at Bottisham. In March 1946 the Tiger Moths and trained pilots left for Belgium. On Snailwell remained a Halifax VI, two Lancasters, a Tempest V and a Beaufighter VIf, all for the use of the technical training section which closed in October 1946.

## Somersham

*TL330770. S of the village*
Near Somersham was established Wyton's Q-Site. Apparently, with enemy activity slight after mid-1941, Somersham was used for practising night landings by Lysander and Hudson pilots of Tempsford's special duty squadrons whose task was the landing and pick-up of agents from continental fields. Little wonder that it was, and remains, cloaked in secrecy. It may well be that very few such training flights were made at Somersham.

## Steeple Morden

*TL302420. 2 miles N of A505, between Litlington and Steeple Morden village*
Those living locally had it all worked out. Since no hangars were visible they were obviously underground! When, by September 1940, Wellington Is, Ias and Ics of 11 Operational Training Unit based at nearby Bassingbourn began flying from their satellite, one had only to 'disappear' to its home station to convince everyone that it had gone to earth.

In the main Steeple Morden was used for circuit flying, leaving the main cross-country and bombing exercises to be flown from the parent station. Then, to add to the tales, the Germans came – unconventionally.

It was a partly cloudy night, one upon which disorientation would be easily possible. Intruder activity was well underway

*Airborne from Steeple Morden, P247 28400 WR:E of the 354th FS, 355th Fighter Group* (RAF Museum P017524).

in the area, and Blitz operations took the Luftwaffe over the region during transit flights. On the night of 15/16 February 1941 the main target was Birmingham. Among the participants was a Junkers Ju 88A-5 of III/KG 1, *V4+GS*, Werk Nr 6214. Quite a new machine it was too, built by Junkers Flugzeugbau MW AG of Dessau and partly by the Heinkel works at Oranienburg. The Luftwaffe had accepted it on 11 November 1940.

Evidently the crew had become completely lost and believed they were over France. They were not, they were over Cambridgeshire when, in bright moonlight, they switched on their landing light. Challenged by a Blenheim crew they fired their signal cartridges and proceeded to land cross-wind over Steeple Morden's goose-neck flare path. As soon as they touched down the aircraft's starboard undercarriage leg collapsed and

the propeller, wing tip and engine cowling were damaged as the machine slewed across the grass. An Armadillo raced to the Ju88, black and with dark green spinners, and the crew of four were soon in custody, dazed by their experience. Unfortunately the Ju 88 was too badly damaged to be of much use.

Meanwhile, 11 OTU flew on, and in 1942 supplied some of the force for the '1,000 bomber' raids. When 11 OTU left Bassingbourn in September 1942 Steeple Morden fell quiet until 26 October when the 3rd US Photo Group came under Colonel Elliott Roosevelt. Runways were laid and hangars added. Then, between 13 January and 4 May 1943, Blenheim Is of 17 OTU used the station, and were afterwards stored here.

In July 1943 the Americans arrived, the 355th Fighter Group flying P-47s. It commenced operations in September 1943, making a sweep over Belgium on the 14th. Thereafter the Group soon switched to bomber escorts and by April 1944 was flying P-51B Mustangs, later switching to P-51Ds and P-51Ks. Its travels took the Group far — to distant Berlin, for instance, and to Karslruhe, Gelsenkirchen and Minden. But it was not merely as an escort formation that it excelled, for the 355th was credited with the highest score of enemy aircraft destroyed on the ground by any Group.

The unit armed its aircraft with bombs and attacked airfields, locomotives, vehicles, radio stations and bridges. On D-Day it gave fighter cover to the Allies and later supported the St Lô break-out. Interdiction and escort duties were continued to the end of the war, the Group leaving for Germany and participation in the occupation force. As well as over 300 aircraft claimed in combat, the Group also laid claim to over 500 destroyed on the ground.

During its stay at Steeple Morden the 355th had some odd companions. The 17 OTU Blenheims may well have been the last Mk Is to have seen much active service. The Americans, ever ready to accept a good thing, had a Mosquito T III here and for target towing a B-26 of ancient vintage. After the war the 4th Fighter Group spent some four months at the airfield.

There is very little left of the station now, but you can lean over a wooden gate which now bars the route which many a P-47 and P-51 took as it crossed the road to dispersal on the north side. Steeple Morden closed on 1 September 1946 and was sold for agricultural use in the early 1960s.

# Upwood

*TL270845. Off B1096, 2 miles SW Ramsey*
On the site of a Royal Flying Corps training airfield, Upwood opened in January 1937. Its four 'C' Type hangars still stand clear on the fringe of the Fens. To Wyton went the RAF's first Blenheims, to Upwood the first Fairey Battles. Underpowered, poorly armed, yet twice as fast as the Hawker Hind it replaced, the Battle began to reach 63 Squadron at Upwood in May 1937, the unit having arrived on 3 March with Hinds and Audaxes. No 52 Squadron, which brought Hinds to Upwood a few days before 63 Squadron arrived, rearmed with Battles at the end of 1937.

The Battle's range was too short to enable it to attack Germany from Britain, and poor manoeuvrability and insufficient armament rendered it useless for ground-attack purposes. Only by raiding Germany from advanced bases in France could Battles be of any use. They stood by during the Munich crisis as a mobile squadron for advanced deployment, but on the outbreak of war both 52 and 63 Squadrons switched to a training role in 6 Group and moved out of Upwood.

They were replaced there by Blenheim Is of 35 and 90 Squadrons, providing operational training for 2 Group. In April 1940 these were amalgamated, becoming 17 OTU which shared Blenheim bomber training for home and overseas squadrons with 13 OTU at Bicester. Daily, the sky around Upwood seemed full of Blenheim Is and IVs, on circuits or training sorties to the bombing ranges off Holbeach. Many who were later to achieve fame in 2 Group passed through Upwood, and sadly a large number would fly only a few sorties before being posted missing. Bostons were tried briefly in 1941.

It was at Upwood that the 'Woods brothers' developed Synthetic Night Flying using a Battle. For this, the pilot was masked and could only pick out the take-off lane by sodium flares placed along its sides. A Blenheim, Oxford and Anson were also involved in the trials, all types used by 17 OTU.

At the end of April 1943 17 OTU left Upwood, to re-equip with Wellingtons. Runway building had then commenced. Halifaxes and Lancasters of the PFF

*Canberra B 2s of 50 Squadron, Upwood.*

NTU used the station from mid-June 1943, but spent some more time at Warboys because of the runway building. The station fully re-opened to them on 1 November 1943.

In February 1944 No 139 Squadron brought in its Canadian-built Mosquito XXs from Wyton for night operations under 8 Group. Part of their fleet was fitted with H2S and 139 Squadron led many night operations marking for other Mosquito bomber squadrons when they operated beyond the range of *Oboe*. From Upwood the squadron flew over 3,000 sorties.

The PFF NTU left for Warboys in March 1944 and was replaced by Lancasters of 156 Squadron Upwood-based until June 1945. These were engaged in the bomber offensive as marker and bombing aircraft, part of the Pathfinder Force, to the end of hostilities. Then No 105 Squadron arrived in June 1945 and Upwood became an all-Mosquito station apart from a few Lincolns here for trials in the autumn. No 105 Squadron disbanded on 1 February 1946 and 139 (Jamaica) Squadron joined 109 Squadron at Hems-

well to form post-war Bomber Command's marker force.

Upwood then passed under the control of Transport Command. On 15 February No 102 Squadron moved in from Bassingbourn and on 1 March 1946 was renumbered 53 Squadron. By then the new arrival's Liberators were joining in the repatriation of troops to India. In March 43 aircraft left Upwood for Mauripur and carried 730 troops to India and brought back 811. By the end of the month the squadron had completed conversion to Liberators and next month despatched thirty flights and brought home 845 men. Late April found the squadron commencing conversion to Yorks and during May the repatriation of Indian troops was completed. The last Liberator returned to Upwood on 16 June 1946 and the squadron disbanded on 25 June.

Like so many stations Upwood needed a thorough clean-up after the war and when this had been achieved 7 Squadron arrived on 30 July 1946 when Mepal closed. Its Lancaster BI (FE) aircraft were joined by others of 49 Squadron, and 148 and 214 Squadrons in November.

During 1949 the three squadrons re-equipped with Lincoln IIs and flew a number of overseas detachments, taking part in the policing operations in Malaya and Aden where bombs were dropped in anger.

No 214 Squadron disbanded on 30 December 1954, No 148 on 1 July 1955 and No 7 on 1 January 1956, as each unit prepared itself for participation in the V-Force. The Lincolns were then replaced by Canberra 2s, forming the Upwood Wing established by first posting in 18 Squadron in May 1955, 61 Squadron in June 1955, 50 Squadron in January 1956 and 35 Squadron in June 1956. In autumn 1956 Upwood's Canberras took part in the Suez campaign.

When the build-up of the V-Force permitted it the Canberra force began to be reduced. No 40 Squadron, which had arrived in October 1956, amalgamated with 50 Squadron two months later. No 18 Squadron disbanded on 1 February 1957 and No 61 on 31 March 1958. Strength was somewhat restored when 21 Squadron flew in from Waddington in October 1958, but it disbanded on 15 January 1959. As a reminder of that squadron's long association with Upwood a Canberra now stands at the entrance to the station, bearing 35's markings. Flying ceased on 11 September 1961.

Upwood now settled down to being a training centre for clerical and accounts personnel. In recent months it has provided accommodation for US personnel and stores, and press reports indicate that it has been earmarked for use as an emergency hospital in wartime. An interesting feature of many of its buildings is that they have flat roofs, which indicates a transition phase of building between the style of the early 1930s and that in evidence on RAF stations built at the very start of the war.

## Warboys

*TL300790. 7 miles NE of Huntingdon, off A141; airfield by road to W of village*
Such was the intensity of Blenheim training by 17 OTU Upwood in 1941 that a satellite field at Warboys had to come rapidly into use. However, nearby Wyton, operational from the start of the war, had just as great a need and so in September 1941 Warboys became its second satellite. For a few weeks Stirlings of XV Squadron flew from Wyton as well as Alconbury, while runways were being laid at the latter.

A new squadron, No 156, formed under Wyton's control at Alconbury in February 1942 and on 5 August 1942 began to move to Warboys to make way for the Americans at Alconbury. From Warboys they mounted their first operation, against Osnabruck, on 9 August. Then they became part of 8 Group's Pathfinder Force still using Wellington IIIs. Their first operation under new control came on 18 August with Flensburg as target. Moments after take-off a flare ignited in Flight Sergeant Case's Wellington and the flares were then jettisoned five miles from the airfield. A more successful flare dropping raid was that against Frankfurt on 24 August, but two Wellingtons were lost. Four nights later Flight Lieutenant Gilmour flying X3728 was shot down, on his 47th sortie. On 16 September Sergeant J. M. Hodgson was near Essen when another Wellington grazed BJ757 and tore its fin. Less fortunate was the crew of BJ617 for, during an attack on Saarbrucken on 19 September, sparks were noticed coming through the floor of the bomber. The crew quickly baled out, then the pilot noticed that the fire was out and landed his aircraft at West Malling.

A memorable night for the squadron was 5 October. On returning from Aachen one aircraft crashed at Gestingthorpe killing the pilot. Another came down at Somersham after its crew baled out. On the way out lightning struck BJ646 and about an hour later its port engine stopped. Flares were jettisoned and near the French coast the crew parachuted down apart from the pilot who eventually belly-landed his Wellington at Manston.

Six times in November and December the squadron set off for Turin, a journey of about eight hours in a twin-engined aircraft. On 20 November one Wellington was intercepted by a Fiat CR 42 biplane which the rear gunner claimed. Less fortunate was Sergeant R. J. Wallace during a raid on Stuttgart on 22 November. Persistently a night fighter

attacked BK315 causing such serious damage that it limped into a crash landing at Bradwell Bay. By the end of 1942 the Wellington was becoming dated for Main Force operations over Europe, although many served long into 1943 and modifications allowed them to carry a 4,000 lb bomb. During their 1942 operations the Warboys Wellingtons attempted 297 operational sorties and fourteen aircraft failed to return.

On the last day of the year three Lancaster Is arrived for squadron conversion. The final Wellington raid from Warboys was mounted on 23 January 1943 against Lorient which was again the target when Lancasters came into use on 26 January. Thereafter they flew as part of the Pathfinder Force from Warboys, making their first Berlin raid on 1 March and taking part in the highly successful Essen sortie on 5 March. Warboys had been raised to full station status on 1 January 1943, and in March that year 1507 BAT Flight began to use the airfield. No 156 Squadron operated from here until March 1944 when it moved to Upwood.

In June 1943 the Pathfinder Navigation Training Unit reached Upwood and some of its Halifax IIs and Lancasters were based at Warboys. When 156 Squadron vacated that station the PFF NTU moved completely to Warboys, on 5 March 1944, continuing to use Lancasters and some Mosquitoes.

Two days later a formation of six Mosquito bombers came to Warboys signalling the arrival of 1655 Mosquito Conversion Unit. This was the organization responsible for conversion of crews to Mosquitoes of Bomber Command. It also used some Oxford trainers for bombing practice and navigational training. By the close of 1944 it was flying Mosquito IVs and Canadian-built XXs, and training crews to use Oboe and H2S. No 1655 MCU disbanded at the end of December 1944, to re-form as 16 OTU. This left behind the H2S and Oboe training commitments which were passed to the PFF NTU, then flying some of the Mosquitoes of 1655 MCU. That duty continued until the war ended.

No 571 Mosquito Squadron arrived at Warboys from Oakington on 24 July, forced out of its base by the arrival of Transport Command. It disbanded here on 28 September 1945, most of the crews being posted to 98 Squadron in Germany.

Warboys closed as an airfield in January 1946. It was resurrected in 1959 as a Bloodhound base for the missile defence of Wyton. The airfield is now cultivated, but the watch office remains in quite fair condition. Part of one runway may be seen at the north end of the field, and sections of the perimeter track. There are also a number of huts to be seen. The best preserved item, is the old D/F radio station still complete with radio masts and in civilian hands.

# Waterbeach

*TL495665. 6 miles NE Cambridge on A10*

Waterbeach is of the Fens. They are inseparable. It stands close to the site of Denny Abbey, and when the land was requisitioned in 1939 there was much opposition, for fine agricultural land was being taken. Drainage was surprisingly good because a base layer of sand and gravel lay close to the surface.

By mid-1940 hangar building was much under way and to prevent the Germans from landing Ju 52s the aerodrome surface was festooned with poles and trip wires. Late 1940 they were removed, then the Germans arrived but not, of course, in Ju 52s. They first paid a call on 30 December 1940, and on 3 February 1941 the crew of a Dornier 17Z neatly placed a stick of nine bombs along the face of the western hangar and damaged the watch office and runway. Intruder activity, though, was less here than at other stations.

Waterbeach opened on 11 January 1941, at the time when a concrete track

was being laid into dispersals cut into an orchard to the south of the flying field. Personnel accommodation to prewar standards was good, and the runways almost complete when, on the afternoon of 19 March 1941, Wellington Ics of 99 Squadron flew in and dispersed around the perimeter track. There was plenty of mud to contend with when it rained, for grass had yet to take hold on the airfield. But the problem on 19 March 1941 when 99 Squadron took off for Cologne was dust. So much was thrown up that only six crews could get away and Newmarket was again briefly used before operations were resumed on 30 March, against Brest. On 9 April the first Berlin raid from Waterbeach was mounted, but only three crews out of seven were known to have attacked. The squadron stood by to attack the *Bismarck* on 25 May and next day searched for the *Hipper*. Six crews took part in the July day raid on Brest, a target they were to attack frequently, and the dusk procession west over Cambridgeshire was something one almost came to expect each day.

In March 1941 the squadron had received the first of a handful of Wellington IIs from which 4,000 lb 'Cookies' were dropped initially on 14/15 April 1941 during a Brest raid. The IIs were unpopular, for engine overheating was encountered and crews considered them a risky invention until proved later to be superior to the Mk Ics.

There were a number of bad accidents in 1941. On May 5 'J-Johnny' took off and crashed north-west of the airfield. A bright glare lit the sky for miles around, but the bomb load did not explode. On 8 December 'Q-Queenie' set off for Aachen. Engine trouble arose and the crew turned back. On final approach the other engine cut and the aircraft crashed. All personnel on the station were ordered into the air-raid shelters. Five of the crew raced from the burning aircraft, then the 4,000-lb bomb exploded.

Berlin was again the target on 7 November, but two Wellingtons out of eight did not return. The only raid attempted cost another aircraft and three crews out of six had to turn back. No 99 Squadron flew its last operation from Waterbeach against Emden on 14 January 1942. By then the squadron had despatched 700 sorties during its stay and lost fifteen Wellingtons in addition to several which crashed during operational flying. The squadron left for overseas in March 1942.

On a grey November day in 1941 a Stirling circled the station. Its landing heralded the arrival of a type always to be associated with Waterbeach. Conversion training for Stirling crews soon began and 1651 Conversion Unit formed in January 1942.

For almost two years the Stirlings droned round the circuit, for landing and taking-off in the large bomber needed skill and a lot of training. The accident rate due to swing on take-off and landing was high, but once airborne safely the Stirling was a delight to fly, as manoeuvrable as a fighter. An overshoot to the west meant an almost certain outcome: the aircraft would trip as it crossed the drainage ditch along the Ely road. Many

times in 1942-1943 one would see a Stirling literally ditched and looking very sorry for itself.

Stirlings stayed, rapidly increasing in number and diversity of appearance until November 1943 when Waterbeach again became an operational station, head of 33 Base from September. On 23 November 1943 the Main Party of 514 Squadron arrived, also 1678 Conversion Flight, both with Lancaster IIs. These aircraft had the built-in ability to carry a 8,000 lb bomb, but usually delivered lighter loads of mixed 4,000-lb bombs and incendiaries. They took part in the invasion support operations aiding the break out from Caen, following with raids on V-1 targets and oil depots. The Mk IIs were gradually phased out, flying their last sorties on 23 September 1944. This meant that 1678 Conversion Flight was no longer needed and it had disbanded after *DS654* landed early on 12 June 1944.

No 514 Squadron had flown its first sortie from Waterbeach on 25 November 1943, a mining expedition. Next night eight Lancasters set off for Berlin and one did not return. Contribution to 3

*Many Waterbeach Stirlings like* W7447 *had served previously with squadrons.*

*Lancaster II JI:O-LL734, which flew 39 sorties with 514 Squadron, seen during a daylight raid in July 1944 (RCAF).*

Group Main Force activities occupied 514 Squadron which, by the end of May 1944, had flown 754 sorties for the loss of eighteen Lancaster IIs. Four of those fell on the night of 30/31 May 1944 when the squadron raided Nuremberg and lost a fifth aircraft in a crash two miles from Waterbeach. That proved to be the squadron's worst night.

On 18 June 1944 514 Squadron first despatched to Montdidier a Merlin-engined Lancaster, *PB143-JI:B*, and the first daylight operation took place, against Domleger, three days later. King George VI and Queen Elizabeth held an investiture at Waterbeach on 5 July, many awards for bravery being conferred. No 514 Squadron fought a tough war to the bitter end, taking part in the raids on distant Dresden and Chemnitz in 1945, and finally it attacked Bad Oldesloe on 24 April. In all the squadron flew 3,500 bombing sorties and another 126 in dropping food to the starving Dutch. Aircraft loss amounted to 45 aircraft.

On 22 August 1945 514 Squadron disbanded then, on 12 September 1945, 47 Group Transport Command took con-trol of Waterbeach. Almost immediately Liberators of 59 and 220 Squadrons moved in from Ballykelly. They were soon operating a surprising assortment of Mks 3, 6 and 8 Liberators not all of which were fully converted transports. Each squadron had sufficient personnel to crew thirty aircraft, their task to assist in carrying 10,000 troops of the 52nd Division from Brussels to the Middle East during October's Operation 'Sketch', and then airlift 10,000 Indian troops home from the Middle East. Phase three involved bringing home another 10,000 personnel from India and the Far East. This was a considerable and complex task, nine aircraft leaving Brussels each day, and with each squadron having a prescribed route. Both Waterbeach squadrons flew the four-day journey from base to Melsbroek, Castel Benito, Shallufa, Lydda to Mauripur whence '59' headed for Chakulia and '220' for Arkonam, thence home via Mauripur and Castel Benito where slip crews were placed. Each Liberator was able to carry 26 troops and 500 lb of freight distributed in various parts of the aircraft.

*Immediate post-war occupants of Waterbeach were Liberator troopers of Transport Command, including this example, AE:R–KL687.*

Once the lift from Brussels ended the Liberators from here as well as other Cambridgeshire bases involved flew direct to Castel Benito, Cairo West, Mauripur, Lydda and home via Castel Benito. If you were serving in the RAF at the time, then you will certainly find those names and places unforgettable! The intensity of the operation soon began wearing down the aircrew and in one instance a crew flew for 27 hours without a rest only to be ordered into the air after only six hours' break in India. Other complaints arose because troops persisted in crowding into the rear of the aircraft during landing, which was highly dangerous. The flights were very uncomfortable yet only after a lot of persuasion did the authorities agree to passengers having drinks and blankets for comfort. The official view was that nothing likely to permit serious diseases entering Britain must be tolerated. All involved were given a wide assortment of medication including malaria supressant drugs for aircrew. Difficult to somehow link such goings on with Waterbeach!

No 220 Squadron disbanded on 25 May 1946 and No 59 on 15 June. In their places 47 Group positioned 51 Squadron which began arrving from Stradishall on 14 August 1946. From Waterbeach the squadron's Yorks participated in regular passenger flights and freight services flown from Lyneham to Delhi, Singapore and Cairo. About sixteen such flights were despatched monthly by 51 Squadron.

November 1947 brought major change for on the 24th No 51 Squadron disbanded to re-form as part of the Long Range Force at Abingdon. Waterbeach then became the base for Dakotas of Nos 18, 53, 62 and 77 Squadrons of the 46 Group tactical transport force. They were soon barely in evidence at Waterbeach, being detached to Germany in the summer of 1948 for the Berlin Airlift, following flying on routes to the Middle East. No 18 Squadron returned in October 1949, disbanding on 20 February 1950. It was this same month which saw the demise of 53 and 62 Squadrons. No 77 had disbanded in December 1949, and their place was taken by No 24 (Commonwealth) Squadron which arrived on 8 June 1949.

The strength of Transport Command

130

*Yorks, including* TB:C–MW263 *of 51 Squadron, replaced the Liberators.*

was diminishing by 1950, and 24 Squadron moved to Oakington by the end of February. On 1 March 1950 Waterbeach passed to Fighter Command which was given the station in place of Thorney Island. In May 1950, 56 and 63 Squadrons arrived at Waterbeach. Meteor 8s replaced the 4s late in 1950.

On 22 August 1950 F-84 Thunderjet escort fighters of the USAF's 77th Squadron arrived for two weeks' training, and were followed by 79 Squadron on 19 September. Swedish Air Force Vampires briefly called in September and the following month saw a few Danish Air Force Meteors here for Exercise 'Emperor'. This was an extremely worrying period, for the British government had quite criminally neglected defence needs. Much has still to be revealed, but suffice to say that the discovery of the extent of Soviet bomber capability caused little less than panic in some 'high places'.

On 13 December 1950 the squadrons at Waterbeach were informed that they would be involved in the Top Secret Exercise 'Fabulous'. For a prescribed week at a time beginning on a Friday each squadron would always have aircraft operationally armed and fuelled and

at readiness on the squadron dispersal. Standby aircrew would sit in aircraft cockpits awaiting instructions, with those at Readiness being fully kitted and awaiting telephone orders. Specifically, no obstruction was to be in the way to prevent rapid scramble for action, to be given through Neatishead, Eastern Sector HQ. At no previous time in peace had such orders been issued to fighter squadrons, for the expectation of an unprovoked Russian attack was deemed to be high. Ensuing years saw many fighter squadrons taking a turn at all-weather alerts under 'Fabulous', their aircraft standing at the protected dispersals. Since that fateful decision in the fearful days of December 1950 the RAF has most sensibly maintained high alert states.

For the high speed reaction demanded the Meteor was quite unsuitable. Behind the scenes the Hunter was slowly evolving and to protect their reputations politicians were demanding that the aircraft industry somehow produce — and quickly — a fast fighter. The eventual outcome was that in order to announce to Parliament in the 1954 debate on the Air Estimates that the RAF had a swept-wing fighter the Swift was forced into service amidst much deep concern.

On a dreary day in February 1954 the station received its first Supermarine Swift, and 56 Squadron tried to make a success of this aeroplane which gave much trouble. There were some bad accidents particularly because the Swift tightened in high speed turns and control was far from easy. The squadron persevered with the Swift 1 and 2 but to no avail in a saga which cost lives and much money. To the chagrin of all, No 56 Squadron fully re-equipped with Meteor 8s in March 1955. By then the specialized Hunter 5, its role akin to that of the prewar point-defending Hawker Fury, was almost available and started equipping No 56 in May 1955. No 63 Squadron in November 1956 acquired the more powerful Hunter 6.

The failure of the Swift had drastically upset re-armament Plan K which suffered from financial cuts and the consid-erable problems associated with Waterbeach's next new aircraft, the de Havilland Venom all-weather fighter. Britain's night fighter defences had for years come in for scathing criticism for the Attlee government had greatly neglected them. Eventually there came the Meteor night fighter, a troubled machine. De Havilland, who lost their Vixen fighter-intruder scheme when the Javelin was approved, traded on their Mosquito reputation, first devising the two-seat Vampire and then a similar Venom. So desperate was the night fighter situation that with deep reservations the RAF accepted the Venom night fighter, and also the policy whereby two day fighter squadrons trained for high-speed getaway, and one night fighter squadron would complete the Wing.

A new squadron, No 253, formed at Waterbeach in April 1955, equipped with Venom night fighters, the three squad-rons comprising a day and night fighter

*Some of Waterbeach's 64 Squadron Javelins in 1961 had in-flight refuelling probes.*

Wing intact until 253 Squadron disbanded in August 1957. It was replaced in September by 153 Squadron which in June 1958 was re-numbered 25 Squadron and continued to fly Meteor night fighters. No 63 Squadron disbanded on 24 October 1958.

No 56 Squadron moved out in July 1959 during which month No 46 Squadron brought in Javelin 2s and stayed until May 1961. No 25 Squadron gave up their Meteors and successively flew Javelin 7s and 9s, staying until November 1961. Crews for No 60 Javelin Squadron trained at Waterbeach in early 1961 left on 25 June for the Far East. No 64 Squadron's Javelin 9s were based here from 27 July 1961 until 13 July 1962. A further change came in January 1962 when 38 Group took over Waterbeach, and in January 1962 Hunter FGA 9s of Nos 1 and 54 Squadrons arrived for ground-attack and transport escort duties.

On the afternoon of August 8 1963 a Pakistani pilot in Hunter *XG264* of 54 Squadron landed at Waterbeach. To him had fallen the distinction of being last man home. He halted in front of my camera, stood up as best he could and saluted. That salute could well have been a tribute to all who had courageously flown from the station. The Hunters left in the next few days for West Raynham.

Flying had not quite finished for, with the runway in good state, Varsities from 5 FTS Oakington flew circuits here until they were withdrawn, and a few similar flights were made by Oakington's Jetstreams. The airfield building element of the Army's Royal Engineers are currently based at Waterbeach where, although the runway remains, along with the original buildings, control tower, etc, flying has ceased and frequent rumours suggest that parts of the landing ground will be sold for civilian use.

# Witchford

*TL520780. 2 miles S of Ely on A10, also visible from A142*

For hundreds of years the isles of the Fens have provided sanctuary and succour. At Ely, close by Witchford, the legendary Hereward the Wake made his stand against the Normans. In the past, when floods came, local people fled to protecting high ground, the Isle of Ely, upon which Witchford stands. Help to the needy was what Witchford's fliers would remember too.

In the late autumn of 1944 the Dutch, seeing the Allies advancing, decided to give them special support. Dutch railway workers in the north of Holland went on strike. By way of retaliation the enemy flooded large areas, effectively cutting off the region of Holland which had virtually revolted. Food supplies ran low, and the Germans thought they could starve the Dutch into submission. Starve them they did, to the extent that the Dutch scoured their precious fields for bulbs and were forced to eat their pets to remain alive.

The Allies had their hands full with offensive action, but by February 1945 felt bound to do something about aiding the Dutch. What could be done? The solution lay with delivery of food to keep the population alive. How could it be achieved? It had to be by day which was clearly hazardous. Thus, a Lancaster and crew of 115 Squadron, Witchford, were detached to Netheravon, there to conduct trials whereby food would be packed in bags in Small Bomb Containers and dropped from low level. This might seem easy, but the food sacks repeatedly burst on impact until the delivery aircraft flew low enough to drop their loads effectively.

On 6 April 1945 practice drops of food supplies, thought likely to be needed by our PoWs, were demonstrated to VIPs at Witchford from varying types of Lancasters. Next day Major R. P. Martin demonstrated the art to Bomber Command officers at Lacey Green, by delivering six SBCs with 1,245 lb of food, one fifth the possible load.

No 115 Squadron flew their final wartime bombing raid against Bad Oldesloe

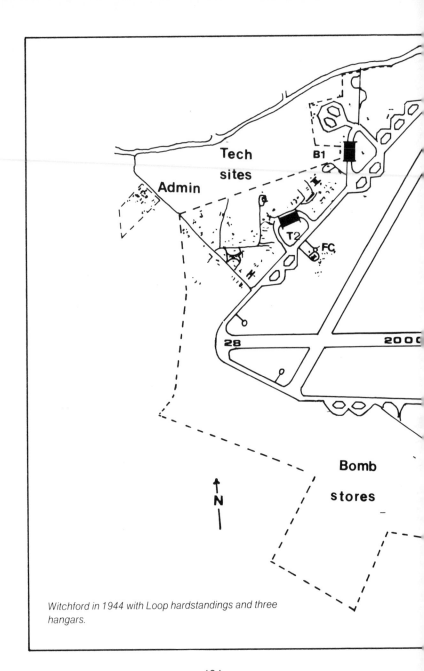

Tech sites

Admin

B1

T2

FC

28

2000

Bomb

stores

N

*Witchford in 1944 with Loop hardstandings and three hangars.*

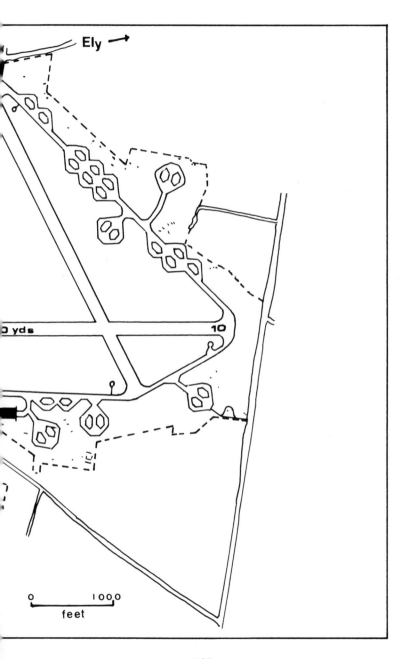

Ely →

0 yds          10

0          100 0

feet

on 24 April 1945. Next day came the first food drop by Lancasters. Each carried five packs of provisions, weight in all 59,551 lb. Weather was clear, apart from April showers, and when the Lancasters arrived over the Hague at very low level there were crowds everywhere. Here was salvation for many, and it seemed the entire city was on holiday. But for all concerned there were moments of bitter disappointment as many sacks burst open upon hitting the ground, dispersing the precious flour. So desperate were some of the Dutchmen that they seized handfuls of the manna to eat immediately.

The following day the Lancasters went again, this time to Rotterdam, and some supplies fell in drainage ditches. As the sacks fell they did so among the people and some were hit whilst others waited in carts and lorries to carry away all they could. One of the saddest moments came when a target indicator from the PFF hit a house, which was soon a mass of flames.

On six more days 115 Squadron participated in the drops, including sweets for children, and tobacco for which appeals had been seen in huge white letters on roof tops. Then, like so many other squadrons of Bomber Command, 115's Lancasters joined in Operation 'Exodus', the return of PoWs from French airfields.

Those supply drops must be something countless East Anglians also remember. My recollection of hundreds of Lancasters truly at roof top height remains vivid, for it was the only time when one saw the might of Bomber Command low in daylight. It was as if the Command was making a fly-past in jubilation that the slaughter was over.

Witchford, as muddy as any airfield could ever be, was just a collection of two 'T' Hangars, a 'B1', three runways and some concrete or metal huts. Placed on the side of the Isle of Ely, its surface sloped considerably, which led to drain-

*Lancaster* KO:U–LL666, *Witchford-based, after its 24th sortie.*

age problems. It opened in June 1943 under 3 Group. No 196 Squadron arrived with their Wellington Xs on 19 July and almost at once re-equipped with Stirling IIIs which began Main Force operations in August. Witchford became part of 33 Base under Waterbeach in September 1943. No 513 Squadron formed here with Stirling IIIs but disbanded before operating. In November 1943 196 Squadron switched to 38 Group and Leicester East, its place being taken in late November by Lancaster IIs of 115 Squadron, the first to equip with radial-engined Lancaster IIs which they operated intensively until April 1944 when Lancaster Is and IIIs were received. Witchford's Lancasters took part in the general run of 3 Group's campaign — Berling, the Ruhr, softening-up for the Normandy invasion. One memorable night was 18 April 1944 when, as the bombers were returning from Rouen, an Me 410 joined the circuit and shot down two Lancasters circling to land.

Three-Flight '115' operated most intensively, despatching 4,601 sorties during 218 operations from which 43 Lancasters failed to return. Bombs dropped included 8,000 pounders and a few 12,000-lb HC weapons for which aircraft were specially modified, *HK698-IL:A* being one such. '115' vacated Witchford in August 1945 and the station closed in March 1946. A 'B1' hangar was used as a storage depot by the USAF between 1950 and 1952. Little marks the airfield, apart from a converted hangar and traces of an entrance by the A10(T) road.

# Wittering

*TF045025. 3 miles S of Stamford by the A1*

'Royal Air Force Wittering, Home of the Harrier.' Certainly both are assured a special place in RAF history. In keeping with its long career the station retains a wide assortment of structures. some close to the road being very old. A 'twin box' watch office and tower was built in

front of three nine-bay 'C' Type hipped hangars, one of which became an awful mess as a result of 1941 bombing. Two remain, supplemented by a post-war 'Gaydon-Type' and, more recently, a small hangar.

Wittering in April 1944 was an enthusiast's paradise. Close to the road rested the captured Focke-Wulf Fw 190A-3, *PM173*, camouflaged dark earth and green and having yellow under surfaces and a light blue spinner. Clustered around it were a Wildcat VI, possibly *JV684*, Barracuda *P9917* festooned with ASV aerials, Hellcat 1 *JV124*, an early clipped-wing Seafire and Fulmar *DR716*. All were with the Naval Air Fighting Development Unit based here. Near these was a rare white Coastal Command Hampden, *AE373*. This was the last complete Hampden that I ever saw and a memorable one for, on its grey-green upper surfaces, it carried an assortment of 'white' stripes which I later learnt were night flying formation aids. By that Hampden was the old Boston III, *AF-Z*, memento of AFDUs Duxford days, and a Corsair 1 curiously painted in dark earth and dark green with yellow under surfaces. Its four-bladed propeller was unusual. A second look at a Spitfire revealed it to have contra-rotating propellers. Surprised, I made a careful check and certainly it had six blades and a closer look revealed it to be *RB179* resting among a group of AFDU Spitfires. One was the unusual Mk Vc dive-bomber *BR372* later to be credited with five enemy aircraft. *MH413-ZD:M* was also there, and a couple of Mk IIbs, *AF:I* and *P8252-AF:E*. Beyond them towered the oft-mentioned Grumman Avenger *FN785* whose *YØP* identity letters were bright yellow. It was to end its life in the Wash. All were fascinating aeroplanes.

Throughout its long history Wittering has been an interesting station which came into use during the First World War as Stamford. Between December 1916 and November 1917 it housed FE 2bs of 'A' Flight, No 38 Home Defence Squad-

*Line-up of Hawker trainers of 11 SFTS at incomplete Wittering* (RAF Museum P014705).

ron. The 35th Wing Headquarters at Stamford included No 1 Training Depot Station, here between August 1917 and May 1919. It had for companion 'C' Flight of 90 Squadron (formed from 38 Squadron) from September 1918 until its demise in 1919. Stamford had by then been home for mainly Avro 504s, Camels and Pups. At the end of 1919 it became a storage depot until placed on care & maintenance in January 1920.

Stamford's resurrection followed the air defence review of the 1920s. Its name was changed to Wittering in May 1924, arrangements being finalized on 1 May for the removal of the RAF Central Flying School from Upavon to Wittering because the former station would be in an operational area, Wittering rebuilt, the advance party of CFS arrived from Upavon on 21 July 1926 and during that summer remnants of the school arrived to open at Wittering, complete, on 17 October 1926. Some of Wittering's existing buildings date from this rebuilding

period, one example being the guard-room whose structure is typical of the 1920s.

The main purpose of CFS was the training of flying instructors. Within its nine years here, CFS operated many aircraft types. Between 1926 and 1931 these included the Bristol F2B, DH 9A, Lynx, Snipe, Grebe, Gamecock and Siskin. In 1931–2 Fairey IIIFs and Bulldogs were used and a Vickers Victoria floated in. Further changes in 1932–3 brought Bulldog Trainers, Hawker Tomtits, Hart day bombers and Armstrong Whitworth Atlases before CFS commenced its return to Upavon on 1 August 1935 and completed the move on September 2 1935. Wittering had been selected as a fighter Sector Station guarding northern East Anglia and extended towards Digby, barring entry to the Midlands.

A new FTS, No 11, opened at Wittering on 1 October 1935 and was here until the fighter expansion programme permitted new squadrons to form. No 11 FTS equipped with Audaxes, used Tutors, had Harts from September 1936, Gauntlets and a few Hawker Furies.

Station Headquarters within Fighter Command formed on 11 April 1938, and No 11 FTS left on 13 May 1938, having been a lodger on a 12 Group station. By this time Wittering's appearance had changed again. A 1935 contract required one 1917 hangar to be retained and three small 'C' Type Aircraft Sheds to be constructed. Main Stores was erected in the centre of the Technical Site.

On 16 May 1938 23 Squadron's Demons arrived. Two days later, 213 Squadron's Gauntlets moved in from Church Fenton. In August, 64 Squadron's Demons were here for the annual air defence exercise. New shapes appeared in October 1938 when 269 Squadron's Ansons were affiliated to 23 Squadron whose camouflaged Demons were seen intercepting the newcomers. A winter conference held by Fighter Command at Wittering brought squadron Spitfires and Hurricanes together for the first time. News was given that 'as a temporary measure' 23 Squadron would arm with Blenheim If fighters, each having a four machine-gun belly tray. Companion squadron, No 213, received its first Hurricanes on 16 January 1939 and reached its establishment of sixteen on 3 March 1939.

At 08:00 on 3 September 1939, with German withdrawal from Poland unlikely, machine-gun posts sited around Wittering's perimeter were manned. Detachments from 213 Squadron then moved forward daily to West Raynham to undertake convoy patrols off Norfolk. Blenheims of 23 Squadron commenced night standbys in October 1939, one Flight being at readiness while the other trained at Digby.

Chester's auxiliary squadron, No 610, arrived to help with East Coast patrols on 8 October and, ten days later, there was a scramble for a possible 'bogey' off Wells. Flying increased when on 21 March, 264 Squadron started detaching

Flights of Defiants for training here and at their advanced base, Bircham Newton. On 4 April 1940, 610 Squadron left for Prestwick. Further detachments of 264 Squadron were rotated but April's main event was the arrival on the 7th of 266 Squadron.

Sudden German attack in the West resulted in the Defiants at once leaving for action. On 16 May 'B' Flight 213 Squadron hurried to France via Manston, ground crews conveyed in a Bombay and Ensign, themselves followed by the squadron's other Hurricanes. Early on 17 May, 'B' Flight flew to Merville in France and it proved a busy day for the Wittering squadron. 'B' Flight joined 3 Squadron for an early morning patrol during which a group of Do 17s were attacked with uncertain results. Mid-morning 'A' Flight arrived, and further sorties were flown alongside 79 Squadron with patrols into the evening. Next day was busy too then, at midday on 19 May, Merville was bombed and the Hurricanes there were scrambled as much for safety as anything else. One was brought down — by 'friendly' anti-aircraft fire, and some Ju 88s were engaged. More patrols took place next day then, early on 21 May, 'A' Flight returned to Manston to operate over France from there and Biggin Hill, to where the entire squadron moved on 26 May to escort Blenheim raids and help cover the evacuation of the BEF before returning to Wittering on 31 May. The station then acquired its first satellite, Easton alias K3 where, from 26 May, No 266 Squadron nightly dispersed its Spitfires with 32 Squadron using the site for night flying.

With the Dunkirk evacuation underway, 266 Squadron's Spitfires moved to Martlesham. They reinforced the Duxford Sector whilst that station's squadrons were away. It was 2 June before, operating from Martlesham, the Wittering Spitfires first patrolled over the retreating BEF, and claimed a Bf 110 shot down and two Bf 109s damaged for the loss of two Spitfires.

Possibly knowing of the station's French involvement, the Luftwaffe first directed its attention to Wittering on 6 June 1940. Lights were on at the Q-site when raiders arrived and dropped eleven bombs near Etton. On 9 June, 213 Squadron went again to Biggin Hill, returned briefly to collect belongings on 18 June, then left Wittering for Exeter, moving not long before Wittering's Blenheims drew first blood.

Around midnight on 18/19 June, a handful of KG 4's Heinkel He 111s, operating ironically from Merville, crossed the Norfolk coast near Wells, were soon in the Wittering Sector and headed for airfield targets. Blenheims of 23 Squadron were ordered to intercept and two of the bombers fell to the squadron, one to Squadron Leader J. O'Brien and the other to Flying Officer H. Duke-Woolley.

During the Battle of Britain Wittering was too far away for direct involvement although its squadrons gave reinforcement support to 11 Group, and 266 Squadron joined that Group on August 12. It was replaced by 'Sailor' Malan's 74 Squadron from Hornchurch, among its Spitfires some aged Mk Is with two-bladed wooden Watts propellers. No 74 Squadron was ousted north to Kirton, whilst 23 and 229 Squadrons made use of K3. Long overdue was replacement of 266 Squadron's aged Spitfires. It came in the form of Castle Bromwich-built Spitfire IIs, first taken into action on 7 September when two pilots over Yarmouth chased a raider, later shot down into the sea.

On 9 September 229 Squadron moved to Northolt, exchanging places with No 1 Squadron. Then 23 Squadron moved to Ford and Middle Wallop on 12 September, night readiness at K3 subsequently being provided by detachments of 29 Squadron, Digby. No 1 Squadron on 15 September provided rear support to 11 Group, patrolling Duxford Sector during that day of intense fighting. Although there were alarms, September 1940 passed without Wittering being bombed.

Two Hurricane pilots damaged a Ju 88 near South Cerney and another pair chased a bomber out to sea, leaving it smoking. A trio of 1 Squadron Hurricanes engaged a Do 17 near Banbury and on 27 October others damaged a Do 17 near Feltwell.

In late October 1940, 266 Squadron gave up its precious Spitfire IIs, reverting to Mk Is. Early on 28 October, four small bombs fell in a field near a Bofors site by the A1. Next day was even more eventful when eight pilots of 266 Squadron, operating with 12 Group from Duxford engaged eleven BF 109s. Hurricanes shot down a Do 17 not far from Cambridge, but return fire pierced the coolant system of a Hurricane forcing it to crash near Peterborough. A chase by 1 Squadron near Sutton Bridge on the following day resulted in the destruction of Ju 88A-4 *L1 + GS*.

On 31 October, with cloud base too low for fighter interception, German bombers marauded over a wide area. At Wittering five alarms came in and in the afternoon a delayed action bomb fell in St Leonard's Street, Stamford, where there was machine-gunning and two casualties.

By November 1940 the future could be viewed with a little more confidence. The appearance of a Wittering Wing comprising Nos 1 and 266 Squadrons was important. They trained with 19 Squadron at Fowlmere to form a 12 Group offensive Wing able also to engage German fighter-bombers over the south-east. At night 29 Squadron maintained standby at K3 where 151 Squadron placed part of its strength from 12 November. Sixty bombs fell near Wittering on 20 November 1940, some at Barnack. Accordingly, No 25 Squadron moved in from Debden on 27 November to engage night raiders and was joined, three weeks later, by 151 Squadron which brought its Hurricanes from Bramcote. For the day fighter role, 229 Squadron's Hurricanes replaced No 1 Squadron on 15 December 1940 and, in the midst of these squadron moves, command of the station passed from Group Captain Harry Broadhurst to Group Captain Basil Embry. No 229 moved to Speke shortly before Christmas so that in the New Year Wittering and K3 housed Nos 25 (Beaufighter), 151 (Hurricane and Defiant) and 266 (Spitfire) Squadrons.

January 1941 was extremely cold. Heavy snow fell on four days, icy conditions making fire-fighting very difficult. A German bomber crew delivered a New Year's Day gift of four 50 kg bombs to the rear of 25 Squadron's hangar, damaging the boiler house and coal compound. A clear, cold night with full moon, 16 January was ideal for fighting — if one could withstand the cold. Contrails from enemy aircraft were that night clear to view over a wide area and Pilot Officer Stevens of 151 Squadron scored his first success, Do 17Z 5K + DM, Werke Nr 3456, of 4/KG 3 shot down near Brentford, Essex. After refuelling and rearming, his Hurricane was off again and Stevens shot down He 111H-5 A1 + JK, Werke Nr 3638, of 2/KG 53 in the sea off Canvey Island.

Another clear night was 14 March 1941. The moon was high when, at about 23:00, a German bomber raced low across Wittering, unloading six 250 kg bombs and about 100 incendiaries on to the camp. The first bomb penetrated the roof of 25 Squadron's hangar, smashed through the wing of a Beaufighter but did not explode. A second bomb burst in the hangar roof, causing widespread damage. The third hit the airmen's cookhouse and the fourth exploded by the gas decontamination centre. A fifth went off by the Officers' Mess, shattering the Card Room and living accommodation above. The sixth burst on the squash court. Incendiaries set a hangar on fire, and burnt in the station cinema and two barrack blocks. Surprisingly, although fires raged for an hour and a half and there was considerable enemy activity overhead, no more bombing took place. Three men were killed and seventeen

injured, two of whom died later. By noon next day the station was fully operational. On 23 March it responded to the attack when, for the first time, Spitfires of 266 Squadron participated in an offensive strike.

At night both 25 and 151 Squadrons were busy when Commander-in-Chief Fighter Command, Air Chief Marshal Sholto Douglas, visited the station on 10 April 1941. Whilst he was there Sergeant Bennett of 25 Squadron destroyed a Ju 88, 151 Squadron scored a victory and Flight Lieutenant Armitage of 266 Squadron a possible. In all seven enemy bombers were destroyed during that night's raid on Birmingham.

Emphasis at Wittering remained on night fighting. Whereas night fighter operations had largely been mounted from the satellite to protect the main base, the opposite policy was now in force. Sophistication of night fighting and radar gear demanded more elaborate facilities.

On 7 May nine medium sized bombs were laid across Wittering's parade ground and on to a corner of a barrack block, five men being killed and ten injured. That night the enemy suffered more, 25 Squadron claiming three raiders. Enemy response seemed swift, too, because, on 8 May, Wittering was twice attacked. In fine, clear conditions, a diving intruder dropped ten HEs and incendiaries killing Pilot Officer Carlin of 151 Squadron and damaging a number of aircraft, one of which was burnt. In the second attack five HEs and incendiaries fell by the watch office. Wittering's night fighters were meanwhile very busy, laying claim to two bombers and engaging three more.

Undaunted, the Luftwaffe returned the following night and dropped four HEs. A burst water main was soon repaired. One bomb fell on a hangar hitting a girder but failed to explode. Pilot Officer Picknet of 25 Squadron landed soon after he claimed to have shot down 'possibly a FW 200'. And still the attacks were not over. On 10 May, last night of the maor

German night Blitz, four HEs and incendiaries aimed at the camp, overshot close to Wittering village. The station's pilots that night claimed five enemy aircraft, although confirmation was not possible. German records list seven aircraft as missing.

As RAF activity over France increased, 266 Squadron was more and more drawn into the fighting, operating mostly from the satellite. On 27 June, for instance, Sergeant Lewis claimed a Bf 109, but it cost two of the squadron's pilots. A fast fight developed on 3 July, two 109s being claimed and five damaged. Next month 266 Squadron re-equipped with Spitfire Vbs. Autumn 1941 witnessed the opening of the second satellite, at King's Cliffe, to where 266 Squadron moved.

Defiants of 151 Squadron and Beaufighters of 25 Squadron were here at the start of January 1942. No 266 left the Sector and was replaced by 616 Squadron, but there was no successor to 25 Squadron which moved early in January to Ballyhalbert. Room had been made for 1529 BAT Flight which formed in January and moved to Collyweston (alias K3 and WB3) in April. Enemy night activity was mainly devoted to shipping operations. Defiants of 151 Squadron patrolling over the sea on 19 February 1942 came across some Do 217s, one of which was shot down by Squadron Leader Smith's gunner, Flight Lieutenant Beale. That night three more Do 217s and a Ju 88 were engaged.

For *Circus* and escort operations No 486 (NZ) Squadron came from Kirton on 9 April, permitting 616 Squadron to stand down for conversion to Spitfire VIs. It also had an unusual night defence role for a Spitfire squadron, since it was affiliated to No 532 Squadron, Wittering's Turbinlite organization. On 10 July 1941, No 1453 (Turbinlite) Flight, the third of ten, had formed at Wittering with a nominal strength of eight Havocs and Bostons each with an airborne searchlight in the nose. The first patrol was flown on 22

October 1941. At first the Flight operated with the aid of satellite Hurricanes of 151 Squadron whose task was to shoot at any illuminated enemy aircraft. On 4 September 1942 the Flight became 532 Squadron whose Turbinlite force comprised two Havoc 1 (T)s and six Boston III (T)s in mid-October, by which time it had its own Hurricanes. Operations had, however, ceased after the squadron participated in experimental flights during which attempts were made to illuminate enemy aircraft by dropping flares. Disbandment came on 25 January 1943, by which time Wittering had achieved distinction for very different reasons.

Basil Embry, never one to be left behind or out of excitement, was greatly thrilled when, on 6 April 1942, the first Mosquito II for 151 Squadron touched down. Only 157 Squadron at Castle Camps had hitherto received Mosquito fighters and Embry was determined that one from his station should draw first blood a claim to success being made on 29 May when, at dawn, Flight Lieutenant Pennington engaged what was listed as a Heinkel 111 over the North Sea.

A new BAT Flight formed here on 23 November, No 1530 which left for Collyweston in January 1943. That month witnessed the arrival of the 56th Fighter Group, USAAF, at King's Cliffe. Insufficient accommodation was available for the American taste and the 63rd Fighter Squadron, under Major Toky, lodged at Wittering along with its P-47s until March 1943 when the Group left for Horsham St Faith. This move took place within a general re-arrangement of Allied Squadrons in East Anglia following the departures to the Mediterranean Theatre and arrival of many Americans. One of the decisions made was to pass Duxford to the USAAF, the aged station being of little operational value to the RAF. This entailed the removal from Duxford of an assortment of organizations. First to leave was 1426 Enemy Aircraft Flight which, although placed at Collyweston, made daily use of Wittering. On 25 March

*Wartime Wittering was home for many a Spitfire including this April 1943 Mk XII.*

the Main Party, Air Fighting Development Unit, under Wing Commander E. S. Smith, and the Naval Air Fighting Development Unit, commanded by Lieutenant Commander B. H. Kendall, between them saw to the movement of their exotic aeroplanes. With armament, tactical and handling trials in plenty, there was little room for an operational night fighter squadron and, on 30 April 1943, 151 Squadron went to Colerne.

Almost at once it was replaced by 141 Squadron's Beaufighters from Predannack. They had come to institute a highly secret series of operations code-named *Serrate*. Using radar they operated over enemy territory at night trying to engage German night fighters, carrying out the first attempts to protect British night bombers. Wittering, into the bomber world for the first time, served increasingly as a diversion base. Spectacular

fighter operations were not a thing of the past though, as was shown on 29 June 1943, when a very long range daylight penetration into France was carried out by two Mustangs of AFDU, flown by Squadron Leader McLachlan, DSO, DFC, and Flight Lieutenant Paige who between them claimed six enemy aircraft.

August 1943 found the Americans once more using Wittering. Accommodation problems remained acute at King's Cliffe when P-38s of the 20th Fighter Group arrived in late August, so the 55th Fighter Squadron positioned its aircraft at Wittering where they remained until April 1944, participating in many operations, including an escort during the first attempted USAAF Berlin raid of 3 March 1944.

Wittering, wartime home for many famous RAF figures, came to be much associated with Wing Commander D. R. J. Braham, DSO, DFC, a very successful night fighter pilot involved with *Serrate* trials in 1943. Yet not all of its heroes are men. Late on 24 October 1943, Wellington *DV839* of 14 OTU crashed and burst into flames. Corporal A. Holden of the WAAF was quickly at the scene and, despite the danger, managed to drag the rear gunner from the aircraft before the fire crew arrived. On 31 March 1944 she was awarded the British Empire Medal.

During October 1943, No 141 Squadron re-equipped with Mosquito IIs and moved to West Raynham and 100 Group in December. As the Americans left in April 1944, the Fighter Interception Unit was arriving from Ford, bringing Beaufighters and Mosquitoes for experiments with equipment and techniques. Some operational flying was involved. By that time Wittering held an amazing assortment of aeroplanes, including some of the first Tempest Vs, a Meteor 1, Douglas Dauntless and the Ju 88C-6, now to be seen in the RAF Museum. Only Farnborough and Boscombe Down could compete where assortment was concerned. Crashes were commonplace for the station attracted battle-damaged aircraft. Flapless, brakeless, seriously damaged, engines out of use, seriously wounded aboard, the station faced all such situations in 1944.

Shortly before the invasion's final build-up, Wittering hosted Auster IVs of 658 Squadron, the first of which touched down on 1 April 1944, the squadron leaving after a three-week stay here and at Collyweston. 14 April marked the arrival from Exeter of another unusual organization, the Gunnery Research Unit which brought along one of the last Fairey Battles, and accommodated itself at Collyweston.

Summer 1944 brought more crippled aircraft to Wittering. Late on 28 July, two C-47s collided north-west of the airfield, crashing at Ketton with heavy casualties. Wittering was used as a night landing ground for paratroops, leading to more accidents. Between the many activities here, 1530 BAT Flight continued flying until disbandment on 1 August 1944. Beaufighters and Mosquitoes, along with Fireflies and Fulmars, served with the FIU and, at the height of the flying bomb assault, tested interception techniques. To place them more ideally the Unit moved to Ford on 23 August.

On 3 August 1944, Air Marshall Sir Roderic Hill, AOC, ADGB, proposed the formation of the Central Fighter Establishment, embracing day and night fighter wings, to the Air Ministry. Liaison with day fighter units would be undertaken by the Day Fighter Wing ensuring the latest technical developments and tactics were appreciated. It would include a 'Fighter Training Unit', arising from the existing Fighter Leaders' School and use Spitfires and Martinets. Also within DFW would be the Typhoon-equipped Fighter-Bomber Wing of FLS. An Air Support Development Unit would be formed, and the existing AFDU re-established to comprise six twin-engined and twenty single-engined aircraft. In the Night Fighter Wing would be a training unit, also the FIU established at twenty twin and five single-engined aircraft. Authority to CFE to form was granted on 4 September 1944 and FLS began moving into Wittering on 6 October. Command was vested in an Air Commodore when HQ CFE opened at Wittering on 26 October and AFDU became the Air Fighting Development Squadron, the layout of the Establishment being somewhat different from that originally envisaged. In February 1945, the elements of CFE gathered at Tangmere.

Although the flying bomb campaign was largely over when CFE formed, launches from He 111s flying low over the sea continued, and caused great concern, when, on Christmas Eve 1944, the V-1s were directed towards Manchester. To guard against extension of such manoeuvres, 68 Squadron moved into Wittering on 2 February 1945, flew its last Mosquito XVII and XIX sorties from

Wittering and before moving to Coltishall on 27 February re-equipped with the troublesome Mosquito NF XXX. With the squadron's departure, the operational wartime career of Wittering ended. Claims by the station's squadrons stood at 151½ enemy aircraft destroyed, fifty probables and 61½ damaged. The FIU laid claim to 82 V-1s. Before Flying Training Command took control of the station, on 31 March 1945, NAFDU moved to Ford and the Enemy Aircraft Flight to Tangmere. Wittering then passed to 21 Group.

The European war had ended when Mr Martin of Martin Baker Aircraft sought permission to use Wittering's runway for trials of his ejector seat using a Defiant, the best aircraft he could prise from the authorities who, suspicious of the firm, offered him a particularly poor example — as he expected they would!

On 17 December 1945, the Flying Training Command Instructors' School arrived from Brize Norton, staying until 24 May 1946. Fighter Command regained Wittering on 1 April 1946. On 15 April, 41 Squadron's snarling Spitfire 21s arrived and on 1 May, 219 Squadron's Mosquito NF 30s. They were preceded by road by an important new shape, the Handley Page Hastings, the prototype of which, on 7 May, flew for the first time from Wittering making use of the station's long runway.

Spitfire 16s of 19 Squadron moved in on June 22 after 141 Squadron re-formed here on 17 June and received Mosquito NF 36s. A third night fighter squadron, No 23, re-formed in September 1946 and equipped with the older Mosquito NF 30, when No 219 was renumbered on 1 September. On 23 January 1947, both 23 and 141 Squadrons vacated Wittering for Coltishall. The other two day fighter squadrons moved to Church Fenton, also in 12 Group, in mid-April 1947. No 19 Squadron had re-armed with Hornet 2s late in 1946.

On 20 April 1947, 264 Squadron arrived to be Wittering's sole occupant and to free Linton-on-Ouse for a second Hornet Wing. Its Mosquito NF 36s were at Wittering until mid-January 1948 when they moved to Coltishall. Flying Training Command resumed control of Wittering on 20 February 1948, the second post-war phase opening when No 1 Initial Training School occupied the station until 6 April 1950, after which activity fell to a low ebb.

Wittering had been earmarked for improvement and use as a bomber station. The 0/26 9,052-ft asphalt runway was strengthened and a new 'Gaydon' Type hangar erected. During the end of rebuilding, the Central Servicing Development Establishment was here, from December 1952 until March 1953.

Wittering passed to Bomber Command in 1953 and, early in August, Lincolns of 61 Squadron arrived, along with others of 49 Squadron. Little was seen of these aircraft for, in November 1953, a 49 Squadron detachment moved to Africa and, on return, went to Upwood. From March to June 1954, 61 Squadron's Lincolns were in Kenya. The jet age had by then overtaken Wittering for, on 12 December 1953, No 76 Squadron re-formed with Canberra 2s. On 25 February 1954, No 40 Squadron's Canberras arrived from Coningsby and, in April, No 100 Squadron moved in. In August 1954, No 61 Squadron re-armed with Canberra 2s to complete the Wittering Wing.

This third post-war phase was brief because Wittering had been selected for the V-Force, for which specialized building took place. No 61 Squadron left for Upwood in July 1955, and No 76 in November went to Weston Zoyland for specialized duties like 100 Squadron at Wittering until disbandment on 1 September 1959. The movement of 40 Squadron to Upwood came in November 1956.

Although a fully operational station, new techniques and trials were traditionally undertaken at Wittering, the Bomber Command Development Unit (a latterday sort of AFDU) moving in during July 1954, at the same time as No 1321 Flight

*'Harrier' and 'Wittering' will forever be linked.*

formed for Britain's nuclear weapon tests.

At the start of July 1955, the V-Force in the form of the Valiants of 138 Squadron, arrived to make Wittering the prime operational V-bomber station. No 49 Squadron followed in May 1956. In autumn of that year, 138 Squadron (detached to Malta) carried out devastating, accurate attacks on Egyptian airfields during Operation 'Musketeer'. The task of participating in the Christmas Island nuclear weapons trials during 1956–7 had meanwhile fallen to 49 Squadron. BCDU wound down in March 1960, and 7 Squadron brought its Valiants here from overcrowded Honington in September 1960.

The disastrous discovery that Valiants were suffering from metal fatigue ended this phase in Wittering's career. On 26 June 1961, No 49 Squadron disbanded, followed on 1 April 1962 by No 138 and at the end of September 1962, by 7 Squadron which ended the Valiant's service here.

Replacement had already come about. Apart from the Navigational Bomb Sight Development Unit, here was based

the Victor 2 Trials Unit from which 139 Squadron formed on 1 February 1962. On 1 May No 100 Squadron re-formed, also with Victor 2s for which the Blue Steel stand-off cruise missile was prime weapon. It was soon phased out because of its limited low level strike capability. No 100 Squadron disbanded on 30 September 1968, followed by 139 Squadron on 31 December.

Wittering joined Air Support Command on 1 February 1969, the resident Strike Command Armament Support Unit becoming the RAF Armament Support Unit on 1 October 1971. By then the whole tenor of Wittering's activity had dramatically altered. The first signs of a vertical take-off era accompanied the arrival, in March 1969, of Whirlwind HC 10s of 230 Squadron. Control of the station was in the hands of 38 Group.

On 18 July 1969 No 1 Squadron arrived. Some Hunters were brought along, but the squadron's main task was to discover the potential of the Harrier, pilots for which would learn to fly the exceptional aircraft of 233 OCU which opened in October 1970 and originated in the Harrier Operational Conversion

Unit. Harriers had little need for Wittering's long runway and soon established themselves world famous for they were the world's first operational V/STOL combat aircraft.

In November 1971, No 230 Squadron commenced re-arming with Puma helicopters before moving to Odiham at the start of 1972. To make fuller use of the station, Hunter 9s of No 45 Squadron arrived from West Raynham on 29 September 1972, and No 58 Squadron reformed as its offshoot on 1 August 1973. These squadrons, 2 September 1974, formed a Hunter Wing which had both training and operational commitments. It disbanded on 26 July 1976, leaving the Harriers in the prime position they currently occupy. Just how splendid the Harrier is was amply proven during the South Atlantic conflict in which Wittering was much involved.

# Wratting Common

*TL645510. By B1052, 2½ miles NE of Balsham, Cambridgeshire*
Astride the East Anglian heights Wratting Common which opened in May 1943, was a typical bomber airfield. Remnants of the station ring to the sound of farm implements on land owned by Lord Vestey, or to the hustle and bustle of a commercial vehicle haulage business. Essential tasks were performed here, but with rather less glamour than at other airfields in the area.

In the general re-organization of Stirling squadrons in 32 Base run by Stradishall, 90 Squadron moved from Ridgewell to the airfield, then known as West Wickham, on 31 May 1943 and at the height of the Stirling bomber's career, resuming action with a mining operation on 3/4 June. The Battle of the Ruhr was being fiercely waged and during June No 90 Squadron's targets included Krefeld, Mulheim and Wuppertal. It took part in the destruction of Hamburg in July and fifteen crews set off from West Wickham for the famous Peenemünde raid. Twice they attacked Turin in August and then

West Wickham underwent a sudden transformation. The station's name had brought confusion with another similarly named airfield, and on 21 August it became known as Wratting Common which really lies just to the north.

Stirling operations continued with less frequency until mid-October when 90 Squadron moved to Tuddenham.

The Ladder Plan, whereby 3 Group squadrons would equip with Lancaster Is and IIIs, became effective in November. To make room for 514 Squadron at Waterbeach No 1651 Conversion Unit moved into Wratting and 90 Squadron had to make way for them. No 1651 CU arrived on 20 November, becoming part of 32 Base.

Stirling training was a costly business, and a very large number of accidents occurred at Wratting, mainly due to incorrect handling on take-off and landing. Basic operational training was conducted as crews converted from twins at OTUs to four-engined aircraft. Most then proceeded to 3 LFS at Feltwell and, when there were sufficient Lancasters in the Group, the Stirling Conversion Unit moved on 10 November 1944 to Woolfox Lodge. In its place in late October 1944 had come 195 Squadron, an offshoot of 115 Squadron, Witchford. It commenced operations on 2 November 1944 with a day raid on Hamburg. Operations followed 3 Group's normal pattern with a concentrated effort against oil targets. Thus Nordstern, Castrup Rauxel, and Wanne Eickel figured prominently in battle orders, along with many other well-known German target areas such as Munich, Duisburg, Dortmund and Kiel. The Lancasters took part in the famous Dresden raid but their most eventful operation took place on 12 December 1944. Witten was the target for eighteen crews and enemy fighters penetrated to 195's leading formation which was broken, a rare event during day raids at this time. Three Lancasters were shot down and another, badly damaged, put down in Belgium. To add confusion fog descended at Wratting and eleven crews landed away.

The final operation, against railway installations at Bad Oldesloe, came on 24 April. Then the Lancasters flew eight supply drops to the Dutch before carrying released PoWs to Tangmere and Westcott.

No 195 Squadron flew 1,367 bombing sorties from Wratting Common during the course of 79 operations in which 6,144.6 tons of bombs were dropped. The squadron disbanded on 14 August 1945 and flying all but ceased here. For a while the station housed some of the personnel needed for transport operations from Stradishall and several Stirling Vs called. Oxfords of 1552 BABS Flight flew from the airfield in April 1946, at which time a ground school to assist 51 Squadron's conversion to Avro Yorks functioned here. The station closed at the end of April 1946 and was then used for displaced persons. Now, a long line of conifers stretch across the one-time airfield whose presence is still marked by a few huts and three hangars.

# Wyton

*TL285741. NE of Huntingdon, at junction of A141/B1090*

Few aeroplanes arrive amid the sort of euphoria which courted the Bristol Blenheim, supposedly able to outpace existing fighters. Sadly the latter were only of the biplane variety. To Wyton came the initial Blenheim for the RAF, inauspiciously completing its arrival on 19 March 1937 with a ground loop. The Blenheim and Wyton have become inseparably linked in history. It was Blenheim-*N6125* which, a few moments after war was declared, made the first Bomber Command sortie, to photograph the German fleet in the Schillig Roads preparatory to a bombing attack. It was unlucky for 139 Squadron that when they participated in that raid the following day the weather and an element of bad map reading defeated their part in the operation.

Wyton became linked with the Mosquito in 1942. From this station in December No 109 Squadron's Mosquitoes first operated *Oboe*, the blind bombing device. Six Mosquitoes of 109 Squadron set out on 5 March and successfully marked the Krupp works for a devastating attack.

Wyton was also the station from where the first Master Bomber operated, Wing Commander J.H. Searby, whose task it was to control the attack on the V-weapons research establishment at Peenemünde. Thus, Wyton's place in RAF history is assured, and it is good that it remains an active station.

It has a long history, the present aerodrome swallowing the small field where in World War 1 a procession of RFC men learnt to fly a wide variety of aircraft types from a site that opened in 1916. Reserve and training squadrons passed through, the aerodrome buildings being on the west side where a few modern buildings stand. Between the wars, Alan Cobham's circus made use of the field.

When building of the new aerodrome started at the end of 1935 the hangars were sited on the south side. RAF expansion brought the first personnel and aircraft to Wyton in July 1936, before the hangars were ready. When No 139 Squadron re-formed on 3 September 1936 an attempt was made to house the Hinds in one of the old wooden sheds. The roof sagged so much when the doors were opened that they could not be closed again. Hinds had to be picketed out until No 1 Hangar opened in November.

On 1 December 114 Squadron re-formed as winter rain was reducing the airfield to mud. Not, however, reducing the area of the old airfield and from there flying was still possible. Old airfields, it seems, were very carefully sited.

On 1 March 1937 Wyton passed to 2 Group and Blenheims began to arrive. Long-nosed Blenheims replaced the Mk Is in 1939 and with these the two squadrons went to war. They flew few sorties

148

**Above** *1914-1918 Wyton viewed roughly along the line of the present main runway* (RAF Museum P4072).

**Below** *Maurice Farman S 11 Shorthorn* N5073 *Wyton* (Captain D.S. Glover, via P.H.T. Green).

*With Wyton's long serving sheds a backdrop, RE 8 A3225 in 1918 (Captain D.S. Glover, via P.H.T. Green).*

before late November 1939 when they moved to France, their place being taken by Battles of XV and 40 Squadrons which had returned to convert to Blenheims.

An expected move to France did not come about and both squadrons were at Wyton when the western storm broke in May 1940. The harshness of battle was at once evidence when 40 Squadron was committed to action against Dutch targets. Appalling casualty lists were opened. The Blenheim's limitations were hammered home on 12 May when half the force of XV Squadron failed to return. This put XV Squadron out of the fight for a few days, but soon Wyton's squadrons were to be seen daily, in vics of three, usually twelve to a formation, heading for

*At Wyton, the Blenheim 1 joined the RAF. K7078 served 139 Squadron.*

terrifying action. The carnage during this period was simply horrific, and all to no avail.

Once France fell both squadrons, using Alconbury for dispersal, settled down to a regular day bomber and reconnaissance role using cloud cover, sometimes flying solo, occasionally in formation. They had been joined in late May 1940 by the tattered remnants of 57 Squadron which had virtually been wiped out in France and which, after re-forming, had been detached to Lossiemouth on 24 June as an anti-invasion measure and for possible operations over Scandinavia. This squadron returned to Wyton on 29 October 1940, when the station's Blenheim days were nearly over..

On 1 November 1940 Wyton and its three squadrons were switched to 3 Group. All re-equipped with Wellington Ics. No 57 Squadron moved to Feltwell, but the other two stayed on although 40 Squadron moved completely to Alconbury on 2 February 1941. Both squadrons flew night raids. From early 1941 No 4 Blind Approach Training Flight, which became 1504 BAT Flight, was at Wyton, moving to Graveley on 5 August 1942.

In January 1941 Wyton had begun to take on greater importance, for Short Brothers established a working party there to support the entry of the Stirling into 3 Group. During March 1941 XV Squadron began to equip with the new four-engined bomber. The change brought big problems for this was an exacting aeroplane. Nevertheless, XV Squadron were not to be trifled with, and when they took the new type into action they did it in style — against Berlin.

The number of Stirlings ready for action was, for many months, small. In the summer XV Squadron tried to sink the *Scharnhost* at La Pallice and at the end of the year raided Brest in daylight.

These sorties were afforded much publicity at the time, but had little effect on the warships. In an attempt to hit them XV Squadron carried out some radio-controlled night raids, but effective equipment was a year away.

The Stirlings operated into 1942, usually from Wyton whilst training was undertaken at Alconbury, a trail of crashes being none too good for morale. Yet it would be very wrong to think of the Stirling as unpopular; indeed, many who flew in this sturdy, manoeuvrable bomber thought highly of it and when they later encountered the Lancaster rated that a frail, tinny contraption!

The next major change for Wyton came in August 1942 with the establishment of the Pathfinder Force within 3 Group. The Stirlings moved to Bourn and in their place on 15 August came Lancasters of 83 Squadron on loan from 5 Group. Their task was to provide part of the flare force for marking, and during ensuing months they improved their accuracy and attack concentration handsomely, developing tactics which culminated in the use of target indicators

*'Bombing up' Lancaster* OL:D *of 83 Squadron* (Douglas Garton, via P.H.T. Green).

in place of flare bundles. No 83 Squadron continued to operate from Wyton until April 1944 and moved to Coningsby on 20 April. By then Wyton housed Mosquitoes.

The first Mosquito came from Stradishall in early Stepember 1942 in the hands of 109 Squadron which arrived on 7 August headed by Squadron Leader H.E. Bufton. Under the watchful eye of Air Commodore Don Bennett they worked up their techniques and made their first raid against Lutterade power station, a calibration operation to test the effectiveness of *Oboe*. Thereafter until July 1943 109 Squadron performed, and during the Battle of the Ruhr both 109 and 83 Squadrons, leaders and backers-up, played a great part in improving bombing accuracy. In June 1943, when 2 Group was shoved into Fighter Command much against its wishes, 139 Squadron at Marham was switched to night nuisance raids and 105 became the second *Oboe* squadron. Then 139 Squadron was changed with 109 to keep the *Oboe* markers together at Marham. No 139 Squadron operated by night on a small but accurate scale into 1944, leaving Wyton in February 1944.

In January 1944 No 1409 Meteorological Reconnaissance Flight arrived with Mosquitoes from Oakington. Their role was as vital as that of any Wyton unit, for each day they gathered weather forecast material to permit planning of the night's raids over the Continent, often penetrating very deeply into Germany and in daylight, and feeding data to both Bomber Command and the 8th Air Force. This they did from Wyton until the end of the war, and flew the vital weather reconnaissance flights prior to the launching of the D-Day landings.

On 15 September 1944 No 128 Squadron re-formed at Wyton and, equipped with Mosquito XVIs, became part of the Light Night Striking Force until the end of hostilities. Expanding the station's capability, 163 Squadron also re-formed here with Mosquitoes on 25 January 1945, disbanding at Wyton on 19 August that year.

The peacetime phase for Wyton began when 156 Squadron brought in their Lancasters. The squadron disbanded on 25 September 1945 but their Lancasters remained at dispersals long after the owners had gone. No 1688 BDT Flight arrived on 19 March 1946, disbanding at Wyton in November.

On 7 August 1946 3 Group MSU, recently established, moved to Mildenhall. Later that month Lancasters of Nos XV and 44 Squadron moved in, and those of 90 and 138 Squadrons came in November. Lincoln IIs replaced the Lancasters and the squadrons took part in exercises and flew overseas in 'Sunray' and 'Sunbronze' exercises improving navigation and mobility. Anti-shipping techniques were practised and in October 1947 No XV Squadron was involved in Project 'Ruby' dropping 12,000 1b 'Tallboys' on concrete structures. In June 1948 No 44 Squadron made a goodwill visit to Rhodesia.

Nos 90 and 138 Squadron disbanded on 1 September 1950 making way for the arrival on 11 September of B-50Ds of the 330th Bomb Squadron, 93rd Bomb Group, USAF soon replaced by B-50Ds of the 340th Squadron, 97th Bomb Group after which B-29s of the 509th Bomb Group were temporarily here. May 1951 saw their replacement by B-50Ds of the 20th Bomb Squadron, 2nd Bomb Group and later that year the 33rd Bomb Squadron, No 22 Bomb Wing did a tour of duty at Wyton. No XV Squadron had in November 1950 departed and No 44 left in January 1951. Since the end of the war Technical Training Command Communications Flight has also been based here and in various guises has remained.

Wyton underwent major change in 1952 the main runway being lengthened to over 9,000 ft causing closure of the St Ives-Ramsey road before, at the end of the year, the PRU began to arrive from Benson. As a result Bomber Command's last Lancaster squadron, No 82, along

*Modern Wyton, from the north* (RAF Museum P017589).

with Mosquito PR 34s and a few Meteor PR 10s of Nos 58, 540 and 541 Squadrons, arrived early in 1953. Barely had they moved in when they were called upon to photograph the East Coast floods, which activity generated over 20,000 negatives. The Mosquitoes were replaced by Canberra PR 3s first placed in 540 Squadron, and later by PR 7s. June 1953 saw three Canberras of 540 Squadron rushing newsreels of the Coronation to Canada and in October a Wyton PR 3, *WE139*, won the high speed section of the London to New Zealand Air Race.

No 542 Squadron re-formed with Canberra PR 3s in May 1954 and joined the high level day and night photo reconnaissance and survey force which was soon sending detachments overseas. No 542 Squadron, however, disbanded in October 1955. At Wyton No 1323 Radar Reconnaissance Flight, which operated Lincolns as well as Canberras, became a new 542 Squadron on 1 November 1955

and moved to Weston Zoyland on 15 December 1955 to prepare for the 1956 nuclear weapon trials in Australia. In place of the RRF came No 543 Squadron, operating Valiants, which arrived at Wyton mid-November 1955.

At the end of March 1956 No 540 Squadron disbanded, followed by No 82 on 1 September. A detachment of 58 Squadron's Canberra PR 7s was then preparing for Operation 'Musketeer' which was to cost it an aircraft shot down by a Syrian Air Force Meteor.

No 237 OCU, specializing in PR training, moved into Wyton in October 1956. In January 1958 its role was taken over by Bassingbourn's OCU. A section of 100 Squadron flying Canberra PR 7s was attached to 58 Squadron in July 1957 prior to taking part in the 1957–1958 Christmas Island nuclear weapon tests. Victors arrived in 1958 for a newly established Radar Reconnaissance Flight which disbanded in 1961.

*Valiant* WZ391 *spectacularly approaches Wyton's runway.*

Primarily a strategic reconnaissance centre, Wyton was very often involved in large-scale surveys and mapping tasks for which the Valiants were ideal. Such work continued into the 1960s when Canberra PR 9s begin to equip a Flight of 58 Squadron. Closure of Watton resulted in the arrival of 51 Squadron in March 1963. It proved to be a turning point in the station's activity since the newcomer with Canberras and Comet R 2s was an electronic intelligence gathering squadron.

The first Victor SR 2 arrived uin May 1965 for 543 Squadron which had long prepared for the event. That year the squadron photographed Saddleworth Moor in the hunt for the Moors Murderers and in 1967 kept watch over oil pollution from the *Torrey Canyon.*

Lone high-level reconnaissance aircraft having become vulnerable particularly to guided weapons, 58 Squadron switched to a low-level PR role before disbandment on 30 September 1970. It was immediately replaced by 39 Squadron equipped with Canberra PR 7s (until early 1972) and PR 9s. As well as survey work it undertook low-level and shipping reconnaissance and NATO duties. With ever-increasing emphasis on electronic intelligence gathering, the Electronic Warfare and Avionics Unit arrived, its task the design and installation of special equipment.

In 1971 51 Squadron received its first Nimrod R 1. Suitably equipped, it made its first operational flight on 3 May 1974. Comet R 2s were retired, one to Duxford, and on 3 April 1975 the last of 543 Squadron's Victors (*XL193*) vacated Wyton. In 1976 51 Squadron relinquished its last Canberra, a B 6, *WT305*, which guards Wyton's main gate along with a long service Canberra PR 7, *WH773*.

More Canberras arrived in August 1975, T 17 electronic warfare trainers flown by RAF and RN crews of 360 Squadron. On 3 October 1978 even more Canberras came to the station from

154

Malta, this time PR 7s of 13 Squadron, to concentrate upon low-level night photography. No 39 Squadron meanwhile was equipped for Infra Red Line Scan and also for night operations.

Since February 1969 No 26 Squadron had been Wyton-based, using Basset and Devon light transports. February 1976 saw its disbandment, aircraft and crews becoming part of No 207 Squadron Detached Flight placed here for the use of RAF Support Command.

As part of the plan to position all the remaining RAF Canberras at Wyton, and following the disbandment of 13 Squadron, No 100 Squadron (which absorbed the target-towing No 7 Squadron) moved into the station in January 1982. Wyton had various involvements in the South Atlantic conflict and on 29 July 1982, No 231 OCU, merely a Flight of Canberra B 2s and T 4s, arrived from Marham. Disbandment of 39 Squadron had come on 28 May, then a few Canberra PR 9s equipped a new Photographic Reconnaissance Unit later re-designated No 1 PRU. April 1983 saw the arrival of HQ 25 Squadron whose 'B' Flight defends the station with Bloodhound 2 ram-jet guided weapons.

Wyton is the only Cambridgeshire RAF station virtually operational continuously. To the uninitiated the Royal Air Force is thought to exist only to wage war, although for many decades its primary role has been the prevention of conflict. The contribution it makes to civilian life is little known, yet it has been and continues to be considerable. In 1961, for instance, Wyton Valiants photographed British Honduras assessing hurricane damage, they photographed Agadir after its catastrophic earthquake and watched the alarming progress of Tristan da Cunha's volcanic eruption. Mapping of vast areas has been undertaken by Wyton's squadron for many Commonwealth countries, and surveys of the British Isles have been undertaken from the station. Wyton's aircraft have also recorded the growth of East Anglia's network of major road schemes and in so doing have often witnessed the use of familiar old runways to provide hard core for new roads. They also represent techological advance the like of which early fliers over Cambridgeshire could never remotely have imagined. A little about those can be found in the ensuing pages.

# DID YOU KNOW ...?

— The first balloon flight over Cambridge, by a Mr Astley, took place on 22 November 1783.

— On 27 March 1784 two balloons left Emmanuel Close, one landing at Cherry Hinton, the other near Chesterton Sluice.

— On 27 May 1784 a balloon was launched from Queen's Villa, Haslingfield.

— January 1785 saw a balloon ascent from the Palace Gardens, Ely.

— A balloon which landed at Fordham in February 1785 caused great alarm to the inhabitants.

— November 1785 witnessed a balloon ascent from Trinity Hall by Mr Poole.

— Parker's Piece, Cambridge, has served several times as an 'aerodrome'. Mr Green made an ascent from here in his Coronation Balloon at the Grand Fête of 8 May 1830, others marking the Coronation of Queen Victoria in 1838 and the 1883 Royal Wedding. 1880 also saw another flight from here.

— The Barnwell area, too, attracted aeronauts whose balloons made flights from the area on 22 May 1829, 14 May 1830 and 28 May 1831.

— In the rural areas around ballooning also took place with ascents from Cheveley in September 1850, Elsworth on 9 August 1879 and on 3 June 1882 from Gamlingay.

— UFOs are nothing new, one being seen over Gazeley on 14 December 1861.

— The first parachute descent in the county probably took place on 20 September 1889.

— The first aeroplane designed and built in Cambridgeshire was the Frost Ornithopter. Construction began at West Wratting Hall in 1867. It weighed about 900 lb., cost some £1,000 and took ten years to complete. Mr E. P. Frost, a Member of the Council of the Aeronautical Society, based his ideas for a steam aerial carriage on a bird's wing. Frost thought he would need a 25 hp engine to achieve flight which at that time meant a steam engine. The engine he obtained delivered only 5 hp and his machine was abandoned under trees in the Hall, where it succumbed to the weather. Its engine has survived, in Old Warden's Shuttleworth Collection.

— One of the last balloon ascents from within Cambridge took place during the Mammoth Show of 1908.

— Another smaller Cambridge ornithopter was built in 1905 by Dr F. W. Hutchinson with the help of Mr C. R. D'Esterre, Messrs W. G. Pye and Cambridge Autocar Ltd. Driven by a 3 hp Kelecom petrol engine, the 232 lb. machine was tethered for flying, each flap of the wing lifting it about two feet above the ground.

— The 1910 steel tube-framed Walbro Monoplane was built in their St Barnabas Road workshop by H. S. and P. B. Wallis of motor cycling fame. Its 25 hp JAP engine managed to lift it a few feet off the ground in an Abington field before it ground-looped.

— C. Wallis, C. Knightley, P. Booth and E. Muller were in 1910 responsible for the 'Chesterton Biplane' shown in May Week, 1910. Made in a barn near the 'Pike and Eel', it was a glider initially to which a 25 hp engine was added.

— Yet another early machine was made by H. W. Holt, a King's College graduate, in the Engineering Labs. It was erected in Harry William's premises in Victoria Park, Chesterton, but apparently never flew.

— In 1910 a biplane was flown from a field where Cowper Road now stands. In the 1930s, where sometimes a fair was held, there was once a flying display possibly in the same field.

— In 1910 Mr Grose and Mr Fairley built a monoplane in a barn at Manor Farm, Oakington. It was tethered for flight trials which were unsuccessful. The aircraft was then disposed of in Hatfield.

— The first aeroplane flight in the Huntingdon area took place in March 1910. Portholme Meadow was then given to Huntingdon for use as an aerodrome from where, on 19 April 1910, the first flight was made, by a Blériot monoplane. Portholme Aviation was then established which in 1915 commenced building a few seaplanes and later produced Sopwith Camels and Snipes.

— The first sight many Cambridgeshire people had of an aeroplane probably came in August 1911 when a military camp was established near Hardwick, by the A45. The aircraft was a Bristol Monoplane piloted by Lieutenant Barrington Kennett of the Grenadier Guards. It was first spotted over Cambridge on the evening of 24 August, causing enormous excitement.

— At about 17:30 on 10 October 1911 a Blériot Monoplane unexpectedly appeared from the direction of Trumpington. Crowds were soon watching and were greatly excited as the aeroplane 'swooped down by the tower of the Catholic Church well below the top of the spire', just cleared house tops in Regent Street and landed in the north-east corner of Parker's Piece. Out climbed Mr W. B. R. Moorhouse (ex-Trinity Hall College) who had set off from Brooklands. He came again the following Thursday. On 29 November he visited Cambridge yet again, this time landing on Butt's Green (the south-west corner of Midsummer Common) to collect some shoes he had

**Above** *Green's balloon ascent, from Parker's Piece, marking Queen Victoria's Coronation in May 1830 (Cambridgeshire Collection).*

**Left** *Mr Green, Jnr, advertizes his fortieth balloon flight, from Barnwell on 8 May 1830 (Cambridgeshire Collection).*

**Below left** *Blimp Betta II in Jesus Grove, 16 September 1912 (Cambridgeshire Collection).*

158

**Above right** *An early Avro leaves a field near Cowper Road, Cambridge, circa 1910* (Cambridgeshire Collection).

**Right** *Moorhouse brings his Blèriot on to Butt's Green on 29 November 1911* (Cambridgeshire Collection).

**Below** *Gustav Hamel's Morane takes off from Cowper Road field for looping on 21 May 1914* (Cambridgeshire Collection).

ordered from Mr Frank Dalton of Bridge Street. Moorhouse later became justly famous. On 26 April 1915, when flying a BE 2 of 20 Squadron, RFC, over enemy lines near Courtrai his aircraft was hit. He courageously flew it to base but next day died of his wounds. On 22 May 1915 he became the first airman to be awarded the Victoria Cross.

— In the September 1912 Army manoeuvres a flying ground was again established near Hardwick. This time there were more fliers, most famous among them being a Mr G. de Havilland and Mr S. F. Cody. Also there were Lieutenant Barrington-Kennett and the naval airman, Commander Sampson. Several other landing grounds were established, notably near Kneesworth where masts were erected for the blimps *Gamma* and *Delta* and at Worsted Lodge where two Short naval aircraft, an Avro biplane, a Deperdussin and 'a Salmson with three tractor screws' assembled. Writing about the event, Mr H. W. Marshall commented that the aeroplanes 'confused rival generals, swept up and down trenches, over every hollow and hedge, highway and by-way, skimmed along only a few feet from the ground'.

— The blimp *Beta II* was placed in Jesus Grove from where it operated during the IVth Division manoeuvres and made a night reconnaissance, finding camps and bivouacs upon which it dropped 'fireballs'. Tempers apparently ran high between Horseheath and West Wickham for the aerial spotters rather upset the traditional activity on the ground!

— In May 1914 Mr Gustav Hamel gave a display in his 80 hp Morane Saulnier Monoplane of 'looping the loop' from a meadow off Cherry Hinton Road where soon after an Army camp was established. Three days later the distinguished flier took off from the beach at Hardelot, France, in a new aeroplane which he had fetched from Paris. He crashed, and drowned in the Channel.

— 1914 also saw a visit by Lieutenant Gathercole, an RFC pilot, who landed near Cherry Hinton to visit relations at the Hall.

— The RFC had a small landing ground just outside Cottenham by the Rampton Road, traces of the landing marker having long remained.

— On 5 November 1929 the airship *R-101* passed over Cambridge during a Royal presentation for the King at Sandringham.

— Just outside the City boundary to the north by Barton Road was a field used for flying displays by, among others, Sir Alan Cobham's Flying Circus.

— On the night of 11/12 February 1941 widespread fog caused eleven 3 Group Wellingtons returning from Bremen or Hanover to crash or force land. Among them was *R1004* of 115 Squadron which, after the crew baled out, crashed into the upstairs rooms of Nos 136 and 138 Histon Road, Cambridge, at 02:45 killing three occupants.

— Shortly before 17:00 on 15 October 1941 a Hurricane crashed into the top room of Nos 55-57 Lensfield Road. The buildings, now part of the Lensfield Hotel, still show the effect.

— A few light aircraft with wartime associations with the county remain active including DH Hornet Moth G-ADKC (ex-X9445) used by 74 Signals Wing, Duxford, from 7 June 1942 to 12 December 1942 when it joined 528 Squadron. Another Hornet Moth, G-AELO (ex-AW118) was used at Wyton between 21 March 1946 and 25 March 1947.

— Both the Cambridge Aero Club's prewar DH Moth Minors were impressed on 9 June 1940. G-AFNG/AW112 eventually became the station 'hack' at Binbrook from July 1942 to 20 March 1943 when it arrived at Wyton to serve there until 26 July. After overhaul it joined the Empire Air Armament School, Manby, on 31 May 1945, serving there until 10 January 1946. It became G-AFNG again on 30 May 1946, in 1954 was converted into a coupé version and is currently owned by R. W. Livett and based at Sywell. The other, G-AFNJ, became AW113 and after preparation served with 22 OTU, Wellesbourne Mountford, from 28 June 1942 until 6 October 1943. It was then briefly at Halton before overhaul and storage. The RAF Flying Club was its first postwar owner. In 1954 it was sold to France where, as F-BAOG, it joined l 'Aero Club Saint Exupery at Grasse.

— One of Duxford's least-known units operated Cierva C30 Autogiros, Hornet Moths, Blenheims and Hurricanes. It formed, as No 5 Radio Maintenance Unit, on 1 July 1940 under Flying Officer (later Squadron Leader) R. E. C. Brie. Its task was the servicing, administration and calibration of radar stations south of the Wash and north of the Thames Estuary. On 21 September 1940 it was re-designated No 5 Radio Servicing Section which on 17 February 1941 became No 74 (Signals) Wing with headquarters at Leighton House, Cambridge. In April 1942 the Autogiro Flight became No 1442 Rotary Flight.

— By 1942 there was a chronic shortage of aircraft to tow targets for firing practice. Evidence of this was unusually shown when on 25 February 1942 two Wellington Ic bombers flew over Cambridge towing sleeve targets. Havocs were also later thus employed in the area.

— The first jet flight across Cambridgeshire was made by a Gloster F.9/40 DG206 as it proceeded from Newmarket Heath, where it first flew on 17 April 1943, to Barford St John. The F.9/40 was the prototype form of the Meteor.

— The first jet fighter to be seen over Cambridge was a Gloster Meteor I, one of four detached from 616 Squadron and then at Debden, and which on the afternoon of Sunday, 15 October 1944 practised combat over Cambridge with a group of B-24 Liberators.

— Q-Sites were fields which were at night lit to look like aerodromes in the hope that German bombers would attack these and not real aerodromes. In Cambridgeshire the airfields and associated sites were Wittering — Maxey, Upwood—Benwick, Wyton—Somersham, Bassingbourn—Barley, Duxford—Horseheath, Oakington—Rampton and Molesworth—Grafham. Waterbeach briefly had a 'K-Site', or decoy airfield attached, at Haddenham.

— A frequent wartime sight was a trailer loaded with hydrogen gas cylinders used for barrage balloons which were brought to the Cambridge Gas Works for filling at a site by Riverside. At the Common end of Parsonage Street the RAF also operated a stores unit.

— AFDU Duxford were keen to explore the defensive qualities of the Halifax bomber and on 23 March 1941 *L9496–TL:B* of 35 Squadron arrived from Linton-on-Ouse. During flight trials on 31 March the undercarriage could not be lowered so the aircraft was taken to its home station for a 'sad but beautiful belly landing'. It was promptly replaced at Duxford by *L9509–TL:O*.

— During the first few months of the war Cambridge was packed with young recruits all wearing a white flash in their forage caps. They were under the control of No 1 Initial Training Wing which billetted them in, among other places, Jesus and St John's Colleges. The main RAF Recruiting Centre in Cambridge was in the Wesley Chapel Hall.

— The first Messerschmitt Bf 109E in Cambridgeshire was one which was exhibited in the Corn Exchange during War Weapons Week held in November 1940.

— Thousands of enemy aircraft crossed the county by night, but daylight visitors were rare. Among the unusual aircraft which came was a Do 215 which strafed Cambridge Airport and surrounds, a Ju 86R-2 bomber making possibly the highest raid by either side during the war, and a Fw 200 Condor which I am certain was held in searchlights during the night raid of 6/7 August 1942 and which, being of Kampfgeschwader 40, was probably controlling its Dornier Do 217E-4s doing the bombing. More common were Ju 88C-2s involved in night intruders against airfields. A Ju 88A-5 dive-bombed the Jesus Lane area at night on 27 July 1942, and a Do 17Z bombed Mill Road Bridge area. In 1943 several Me 410 intruders passed over high, and 1944 brought the curious, heavy sound of He 177s.

— The only flying boat to land in Cambridgeshire was a Catalina IVa

*JX224-KK:B VINGTOR IV* of No 333 (Norwegian) Squadron which forced landed intact on 10 August 1945 in a field about 200 yd south-east of the Huntingdon Road/Longstanton junction.

— An unusual site for the repair of Blenheims was established at a small garage on the Huntingdon road at Hemingford Abbots.

— At the outbreak of war Castle Hill House, Huntingdon, was requisitioned and became the headquarters of No 2 (Bomber) Group. From August 1942 to the end of hostilities it served as HQ No 8 (Bomber) Group which controlled the Pathfinder Force. No 3 (Bomber) Group had its wartime headquarters at Exning. Between 20 August 1943 and October 1945 the 66th Fighter Wing, US 8th AF, had its HQ at Sawston Hall.

— Sebro was a special organization set up to repair Stirling bombers. Originally occupying a small part of Trinity College, it moved to a site by Madingley Road where hundreds of wrecked Stirlings were brought for repair and reconstruction. Re-erection and flight testing was carried out from Bourn.

— One of the most fascinating aircraft 'dumps' in the whole country most surely have been that of Richard Duce, established in 1948 by Newmarket Road opposite the gas works. There could be seen among others two Heinkel He 111D prewar bombers still in prewar markings, a Ju 87B, Mitsubishi 'Zero', Whitley III and a host of others even then of great rarity. The site also became the resting place of the last remains of the Swifts of 56 Squadron. Some of us enquired about the cost of a He 111D — the owner wanted £25, but we just did not have the space to accommodate it!

— Summer eves in 1941 and 1942 were frequently accompanied by a pair of very high-flying Douglas Havocs. These, often contrailing, were from No 161 (Special Duties) Squadron, Tempsford, and by flying high were able to receive and transmit messages to agents and resistance forces in Europe.

— Tricycle undercarriage aircraft were rare until the middle of the war. Among the first to be seen hereabouts were General Aircraft Cygnets and the sole Owlet which were used at Duxford to train pilots to fly the Bell Airacobra, only one squadron of which ever formed within the RAF.

— The first USAAF aircraft to fly over Cambridge was, almost without doubt, a Boeing B-17E of the 97th Bombardment Group which circled the town at 17:00 on 24 July 1942

— There are very few types of RAF and naval aircraft which have not flown over Cambridgeshire. My own diaries show first wartime sightings of the types listed here on the dates following: Vought

Chesapeake (12.8.40), Martin Maryland (22.3.41), Beechcraft C-17 (12.5.41), Grumman Martlet (27.12.40), Curtiss Tomahawk (20.2.41), Liberator B II (1.1.42), Wellington GR VIII in white scheme (7.2.42), Vultee Vigilant (2.3.42), Hawker Hector towing a Hotspur II which landed at Cambridge (14.4.42), Spitfire IX (30.4.42), Caudron Simoun (2.5.42), Wellington VI in PR finish (7.5.42), Stampe SV 4 flying at Duxford (10.5.42), Vought Kingfisher landplane (7.6.42), Stearman A-75N3 in RAF markings — very rare (6.7.42), W4050, the prototype Mosquito (28.7.42), RAF Mitchell (31.7.42), Lockheed P-38 (4.8.42), Halifax towing a prototype Hamilcar (16.8.42), Saro London II flying-boat—first time in wartime (20.8.42), Brewster Bermuda (29.8.42), North American B-25C (8.9.42), Consolidated B-24D (13.9.42), Boeing B-17F (26.9.42), Piper L-4 Cub (14.12.42), Cessna C-78 Bobcat (19.6.43), B-24H (27.8.43) USAAF P-51B (25.9.43), RAF Dakota (6.11.43), Sea Otter (6.11.43), Noorduyn C-64 (29.1.44), Vultee L-5 Sentinel (29.1.44), unpainted USAAF aircraft, P-51B, (26.3.44), Boeing 247D (4.4.44), Wellington jet engine test bed (21.7.44), Warwick Freighter (10.8.44), Lockheed PV-1 (13.9.44), Miles Magister II (21.11.44), and Shetland flying boat demonstrated to Sebro at Bourn on 7.9.45 and the largest aircraft seen to that date over Cambridge. Other large aircraft to have flown over are the Brabazon 1 (once), B-36s and RB-36s and, of course, C-5 Galaxies in recent times.

— Just after the war a number of ex-German aircraft were seen over Cambridge, including a Ju 88G-6 on 15 October 1945. More fascinating was the Fw 200C-4 used as a personal transport by Heinrich Himmler, and which called at Marshall's on the morning of 7 July 1945. But nothing could eclipse the stupendous sight of the six-engined Bv 222C-No 012 which slowly crossed over Cambridge on 17 July 1945 as it made its way from Norway to Calshot. Surely, one of the most excitement-generating sights of all time!

— Nine types of RAF aircraft have seen their introduction to service in the county — the Airacrobra, Battle, Blenheim, Jetstream, Mosquito night fighter, Spitfire, Stirling, Swift and Typhoon.

— A very familiar wartime sight in Cambridge was a '60-footer' alias 'Queen Mary' low-loader carrying a dismembered aircraft to 54 MU. That unit formed on 1 September 1939 at Henlow as No 3 Salvage Centre. It arrived at Cambridge on 23 September and established a small depot for wrecked aircraft near Barnwell Bridge, opposite the railway station there. The first item to arrive was a Blenheim IF, and by 21 October 26 aircraft had been dealt with. On 10 November 1939 it moved to its headquarters site opposite the Borough Cemetery where a Bellman hangar, etc, were erected. An early arrival was a crashed Vildebeest then on 7 December 54 MU attended to the wreck of the Heinkel He 115 on Sheringham's shore and via Cambridge took it to Orfordness. Soon the assortment of wrecked aircraft was astonishing, the highlight undoubtedly being the arrival of three dismembered Fokker T8-W floatplanes. So many crashed aircraft needed attention that late in 1943 a large dump of parts from which metal was to be salvaged was established on the eastern side of Teversham Lane. A second huge metal production unit was established where Priory School and the new bypass road are now sited. Rarest items there were several Handley Page Herefords (eg, *L6060,L6082*) and the wooden Dessoutter II *HM507* (ex-*G-AAZI*) which had taken part in the 1934 McRobertson Air Race. No 54 MU moved to Newmarket between 1 and 10 March 1945, leaving behind huge quantities of metal.

— So very much a part of the Cambridge aviation scene has been the Tiger Moth that as a closing item surely one must recall the well-known examples operated since the war by Marshall. The first, *G-ACDG*, had escaped impressment and came from the de Havilland Flying School. *G-AGYV* saw war service from June 1941 to January 1943 at Bircham Newton. *G-AGZY* served at Downham Market from May to November 1943 when it moved to Little Snoring and stayed until September 1944. The others which wore the familiar silver and Cambridge Blue finish were *G-AGYU*, *G-AGYW*, *G-AHLS*, *G-AHMK*, *G-AHUB*, *G-AHXN*, *G-AHXO*, *G-AIBN*, *G-AIZF* and *G-ALTW* and *G-ANFI* all having no local war service.

# INDEX